ELIZABETH BARRETT
BROWNING

Selected
Poems

ELIZABETH
BARRETT
BROWNING

Selected
Poems

GRAMERCY BOOKS
New York • Avenel

This 1995 edition is published by Gramercy Books,
distributed by Random House Value Publishing, Inc.,
40 Engelhard Avenue,
Avenel, New Jersey 07001.

Random House
New York • Toronto • London • Sydney • Auckland

Printed and bound in the United States

Library of Congress Cataloging-in-Publication Data

Browning, Elizabeth Barrett 1806–1861
[Poems. Selections]
Elizabeth Barrett Browning: selected poems
p.   cm.
ISBN: 0-517-12366-5
I. Title.
PR4182   1995
821'.8—dc20   94-40658   CIP

8 7 6 5 4 3 2

CONTENTS

Introduction   9

Early Poems

SONG   15
THE SEA-MEW   16
A SEASIDE WALK   18
COWPER'S GRAVE   20

From Poems of 1844

THE SOUL'S EXPRESSION   27
LADY GERALDINE'S COURTSHIP   28
THE LADY'S YES   54
THE LOST BOWER   56
THE CRY OF THE CHILDREN   72
TO FLUSH, MY DOG   78
THAT DAY   83
LOVED ONCE   84
CATARINA TO CAMOENS   87
THE ROMANCE OF THE SWAN'S NEST   93
THE DEAD PAN   97

From Poems of 1850

HECTOR IN THE GARDEN   105
FLUSH OR FAUNUS   110
MOUNTAINEER AND POET   111
HIRAM POWERS' GREEK SLAVE   112
LIFE   113

A SABBATH MORNING AT SEA 114

A WOMAN'S SHORTCOMINGS 117

A MAN'S REQUIREMENTS 119

CHANGE UPON CHANGE 121

A DENIAL 122

QUESTION AND ANSWER 124

Sonnets from the Portuguese

"I THOUGHT ONCE HOW THEOCRITUS HAD
SUNG" 127

"BUT ONLY THREE IN ALL GOD'S UNIVERSE" 127

"UNLIKE ARE WE, UNLIKE, O PRINCELY HEART!" 128

"THOU HAST THY CALLING TO SOME PALACE
FLOOR" 128

"I LIFT MY HEAVY HEART UP SOLEMNLY" 129

"GO FROM ME. YET I FEEL THAT I SHALL
STAND" 129

"THE FACE OF ALL THE WORLD IS CHANGED, I
THINK" 130

"WHAT CAN I GIVE THEE BACK, O LIBERAL" 130

"CAN IT BE RIGHT TO GIVE WHAT I CAN GIVE?" 131

"YET, LOVE, MERE LOVE, IS BEAUTIFUL INDEED" 131

"AND THEREFORE IF TO LOVE CAN BE DESERT" 132

"INDEED THIS VERY LOVE WHICH IS MY BOAST" 132

"AND WILT THOU HAVE ME FASTEN INTO SPEECH" 133

"IF THOU MUST LOVE ME, LET IT BE FOR NAUGHT" 133

"ACCUSE ME NOT, BESEECH THEE, THAT I WEAR" 134

"AND YET, BECAUSE THOU OVERCOMEST SO" 134

"MY POET, THOU CANST TOUCH ON ALL THE
NOTES" 135

"I NEVER GAVE A LOCK OF HAIR AWAY" 135

"THE SOUL'S RIALTO HATH ITS MERCHANDISE" 136

"BELOVÈD, MY BELOVÈD, WHEN I THINK" 136

"SAY OVER AGAIN, AND YET ONCE OVER AGAIN" 137

"WHEN OUR TWO SOULS STAND UP ERECT AND
STRONG" 137

"IS IT INDEED SO? IF I LAY HERE DEAD" 138
"LET THE WORLD'S SHARPNESS, LIKE A CLASPING
    KNIFE" 138
"A HEAVY HEART, BELOVÈD, HAVE I BORNE" 139
"I LIVED WITH VISIONS FOR MY COMPANY" 139
"MY OWN BELOVÈD, WHO HAS LIFTED ME" 140
"MY LETTERS! ALL DEAD PAPER, MUTE AND
    WHITE!" 140
"I THINK OF THEE!—MY THOUGHTS DO TWINE
    AND BUD" 141
"I SEE THINE IMAGE THROUGH MY TEARS
    TONIGHT" 141
"THOU COMEST! ALL IS SAID WITHOUT A WORD." 142
"THE FIRST TIME THAT THE SUN ROSE ON
    THINE OATH" 142
"YES, CALL ME BY MY PET-NAME! LET ME HEAR" 143
"WITH THE SAME HEART, I SAID, I'LL ANSWER
    THEE" 143
"IF I LEAVE ALL FOR THEE, WILT THOU
    EXCHANGE" 144
"WHEN WE MET FIRST AND LOVED, I DID NOT
    BUILD" 144
"PARDON, OH, PARDON, THAT MY SOUL SHOULD
    MAKE" 145
"FIRST TIME HE KISSED ME, HE BUT ONLY
    KISSED" 145
"BECAUSE THOU HAST THE POWER AND OWN'ST
    THE GRACE" 146
"OH, YES! THEY LOVE THROUGH ALL THIS
    WORLD OF OURS!" 146
"I THANK ALL WHO HAVE LOVED ME IN THEIR
    HEARTS" 147
"MY FUTURE WILL NOT COPY FAIR MY PAST—" 147
"HOW DO I LOVE THEE? LET ME COUNT THE
    WAYS." 148
"BELOVÈD, THOU HAST BROUGHT ME MANY
    FLOWERS" 148

From Casa Guidi Windows

FROM PART I   151
FROM PART II   154

From Aurora Leigh

FROM BOOK II   159
FROM BOOK VII   162
FROM BOOK IX   163

From Last Poems

A FALSE STEP   167
LORD WALTER'S WIFE   169
BIANCA AMONG THE NIGHTINGALES   174
AMY'S CRUELTY   179
DE PROFUNDIS   182

Index of Titles and First Lines   187

INTRODUCTION

Elizabeth Barrett Browning was born near Durham, England, on March 6, 1806, the eldest of Mary and Edward Boulton Barrett's twelve children. She grew up in Hope End, the magnificent family home built in the Turkish style by her father near Ledbury in Herefordshire. The family was well-to-do, owning sugar plantations in Jamaica, and Elizabeth had a comfortable and happy childhood. She began to write verse at an early age; her earliest known poem was written when she was eight for her mother's birthday. Her father paid to have *The Battle of Marathon,* Elizabeth's homage to epic Greek poetry, privately printed as a present for her fifteenth birthday. Her poems also began to appear in such prominent literary periodicals of the day as the *New Monthly Magazine.* But at this time her health began to decline. During her recovery from measles she developed a "nervous disorder" that her doctors were never able to diagnose. In addition, her lungs weakened considerably. Because of her illness, she became reclusive, concentrating on her studies and her poetry.

Elizabeth's seclusion intensified with the sudden death of her mother in 1828. Bad luck continued to plague the family when four years later a reversal in the family's fortune—the abolition of slavery caused a decrease in revenues from the sugar plantations—forced her father to sell Hope End. After several years at Sidmouth, Devonshire, the family settled in 1837 in a house at 50 Wimpole Street in London, where the damp climate caused Elizabeth's lungs to hemorrhage. For treatment her doctors sent her to Torquay, where, it was hoped, the sea air would improve her health. But in 1840 came the worst blow of all when her beloved younger brother Edward—nicknamed "Bro"—drowned in a boating accident while visiting her. Elizabeth plunged into immeasurable grief and guilt, since it was she who had persuaded her father to allow her brother to visit (the poem "De Profundis" details her emotional turmoil at this tragic moment in her life). She spent the next three months in shocked seclusion in her room. She began to rely on heavy doses of the laudanum—an opium derivative—and morphine prescribed by her doctors to ease her physical and emotional distress—drugs upon which she became dependent for the rest of her life. The laudanum induced in her morbid musings that prompted her to wish for death: "Death has such a pleading tongue in what is called its silence." She did not die, however, and in 1841 she returned to London. There she confined herself to her room, which she called her "hermitage" or "prison," and where she single-mindedly labored on her poems, essays, and letters to friends.

A major turning point in Elizabeth's poetic career came in 1844 with the publication of *Poems,* a two-volume collection of her verse. It won her critical praise and established her reputation, as well as the ardent notice of a little-known young poet, six years her junior. In "Lady Geraldine's Courtship," one of the poems in the collection, Lady Geraldine is reading a poem by Robert Browning. In a letter to Elizabeth the young poet wrote: "I love your verse with all my heart, dear Miss Barrett . . . and I love you too." Thus began one of the most famous courtships and romances in English literature, the essence of which Elizabeth captured in *Sonnets from the Portuguese,* which remain among the most popular love poems in the English language.

Robert and Elizabeth corresponded for five months before they finally met on May 20, 1845. Although they immediately fell in love, they did not marry for sixteen months. The chief obstacle was Elizabeth's father, a pious and strong-willed man, who tried to block the marriage of each of his children. On September 12, 1846, while her family was away, Elizabeth married Robert at Saint Marylebone Parish Church. One week later she left for Italy with her new husband. Her father wrote her a vicious and condemning letter in which he disinherited her. Although she tried several times to reconcile with him, she never saw him again.

Elizabeth Barrett Browning's life in Italy contrasted remarkably with her years in England, where she had led the reclusive existence of an invalid sheltered by her domineering father. The move to the warm and sunny climate of Italy symbolized a rebirth where she began to know life from experience rather than from books. Although the Brownings traveled extensively, they resided primarily in the Casa Guidi in Florence. She recovered her health sufficiently to give birth to a son—Pen, her only child—on March 9, 1849. The new climate was also conducive to poetic inspiration. She wrote *Casa Guidi Windows,* which was published in 1856, an overtly political poem in support of the Italian nationalist movement and the events she witnessed while living in Florence. That same year also saw the publication of *Aurora Leigh,* her greatest popular success and the work that made her a true celebrity. One of her most experimental works, a "novel-poem" whose heroine was a female poet like herself, *Aurora Leigh* created a controversy in Victorian England with its depiction of out-of-wedlock motherhood.

The fifteen years the Brownings spent in Italy were rich and full, and the marriage was a happy one. Although Elizabeth's health had improved for a while, after a fourth miscarriage she began a decline from which she never recovered. The slightest bad weather caused severe infections in her lungs, and she grew weaker and weaker. On June 29, 1861, at the age of fifty-five, she died in her husband's arms. Her last word to him was: "Beautiful."

Today, Elizabeth Barrett Browning's poetic accomplishment and reputation lie in the shadow of her husband, Robert Browning, who is considered one of the greatest poets of the nineteenth century. When they met, however, it was Elizabeth who was the more famous. She was England's first truly notable women poet. In 1850, after the death of William Wordsworth, it was she who was considered to replace him as England's Poet

Laureate. At the time, Robert was an obscure avant-garde poet. That same year, the editors of *The Athenaeum* wrote that she was "probably, of her sex, the first imaginative writer England has produced in any age—she is, beyond comparison, the first poetess of her own." This was high praise, even with the sexist qualifier.

This collection brings together Elizabeth Barrett Browning's finest poetry, much of which has been unjustly neglected. She was a versatile poet who experimented with many different forms of verse—lyrics, blank verse, ballads and sonnets—and whose subjects show that she was deeply concerned with the liberal and humanitarian causes of her day. In response to the exploitation of children employed in coal mines and factories, she wrote one of her most famous poems, *The Cry of the Children*. In addition to excerpts from *Casa Guidi* and *Aurora Leigh*, her *Sonnets from the Portuguese*, the sonnet sequence tracing her love affair with Robert Browning, is included here in its entirety. Her husband regarded these as the finest sonnets written after Shakespeare's. The psychological realism and subtlety mastered by Elizabeth Barrett Browning in her sonnets are also evident in such lesser-known late works as "Lord Walter's Wife" and "Bianca among the Nightingales," in which she further explores, quite candidly, the tensions in relationships between men and women.

The poems in this volume reveal Elizabeth Barrett Browning's breadth and intellectual originality. In the 1970s, the Feminist Movement spurred a revival of interest in works like *Aurora Leigh*, and Browning's reputation has since been on the rise. As one of the few nineteenth-century women poets to achieve fame and recognition in her lifetime, she is again being recognized for the importance of her literary accomplishments and the example she set for women who came after her. Her impassioned idealism, her professionalism, and her determination continue to inspire.

CHRISTOPHER MOORE

New York
1995

Early Poems

SONG

Weep, as if you thought of laughter!
Smile, as tears were coming after!
Marry your pleasures to your woes;
And think life's green well worth its rose!

No sorrow will your heart betide,
Without a comfort by its side;
The sun may sleep in his seabed,
But you have starlight overhead.

Trust not to Joy! the rose of June,
When opened wide, will wither soon;
Italian days without twilight
Will turn them suddenly to night.

Joy, most changeful of all things,
Flits away on rainbow wings;
And when they look the gayest, know,
It is that they are spread to go!

THE SEA-MEW

I

How joyously the young sea-mew
Lay dreaming on the waters blue
Whereon our little bark had thrown
A little shade, the only one,
But shadows ever man pursue.

II

Familiar with the waves and free
As if their own white foam were he,
His heart upon the heart of ocean
Lay learning all its mystic motion,
And throbbing to the throbbing sea.

III

And such a brightness in his eye
As if the ocean and the sky
Within him had lit up and nursed
A soul God gave him not at first,
To comprehend their majesty.

IV

We were not cruel, yet did sunder
His white wing from the blue waves under,
And bound it, while his fearless eyes
Shone up to ours in calm surprise,
As deeming us some ocean wonder.

V

We bore our ocean bird unto
A grassy place where he might view

The flowers that curtsey to the bees,
The waving of the tall green trees,
The falling of the silver dew.

VI

But flowers of earth were pale to him
Who had seen the rainbow fishes swim;
And when earth's dew around him lay
He thought of ocean's wingèd spray,
And his eye waxèd sad and dim.

VII

The green trees round him only made
A prison with their darksome shade;
And drooped his wing, and mournèd he
For his own boundless glittering sea—
Albeit he knew not they could fade.

VIII

Then One her gladsome face did bring,
Her gentle voice's murmuring,
In ocean's stead his heart to move
And teach him what was human love:
He thought it a strange mournful thing.

IX

He lay down in his grief to die,
(First looking to the sea-like sky
That hath no waves) because, alas!
Our human touch did on him pass,
And with our touch, our agony.

A SEASIDE WALK

I

We walked beside the sea
After a day which perished silently
Of its own glory—like the Princess weird
Who, combating the Genius, scorched and seared,
Uttered with burning breath, "Ho! victory!"
And sank adown an heap of ashes pale.
    So runs the Arab tale.

II

The sky above us showed
An universal and unmoving cloud,
On which the cliffs permitted us to see
Only the outline of their majesty,
As masterminds, when gazed at by the crowd!
And, shining with a gloom, the water gray
    Swang in its moon-taught way.

III

Nor moon, nor stars were out.
They did not dare to tread so soon about,
Though trembling, in the footsteps of the sun.
The light was neither night's nor day's, but one
Which, lifelike, had a beauty in its doubt:
And Silence's impassioned breathings round
    Seemed wandering into sound.

IV

O solemn-beating heart
Of nature! I have knowledge that thou art

Bound unto man's by cords he cannot sever—
And, what time they are slackened by him ever.
So to attest his own supernal part,
Still runneth thy vibration fast and strong,
   The slackened cord along.

V

   For though we never spoke
Of the gray water and the shaded rock,
Dark wave and stone unconsciously were fused
Into the plaintive speaking that we used
Of absent friends and memories unforsook;
And, had we seen each other's face, we had
   Seen haply, each was sad.

COWPER'S GRAVE

It is a place where poets crowned may
 feel the heart's decaying;
It is a place where happy saints may weep
 amid their praying;
Yet let the grief and humbleness as low as
 silence languish:
Earth surely now may give her calm to
 whom she gave her anguish.

II

O poets, from a maniac's tongue was
 poured tim deathless singing!
O Christians, at your cross of hope a hope—
 less hand was clinging!
O men, this man in brotherhood your weary
 paths beguiling,
Groaned inly while he taught you peace,
 and died while ye were smiling!

III

And now, what time ye all may read
 through dimming tears his story,
How discord on the music fell and darkness
 on the glory,
And how when, one by one, sweet sounds
 and wandering lights departed,
He wore no less a loving face because so
 brokenhearted,

IV

He shall be strong to sanctify the poet's
    high vocation,
And bow the meekest Christian down in
    meeker adoration;
Nor ever shall he be, in praise, by wise or
    good forsaken,
Named softly as the household name of
    one whom God hath taken.

V

With quiet sadness and no gloom I learn
    to think upon him,
With meekness that is gratefulness to God
    whose heaven hath won him,
Who suffered once the madness-cloud to
    his own love to blind him,
But gently led the blind along where
    breath and bird could find him;

VI

And wrought within his shattered brain
    such quick poetic senses
As hills have language for, and stars,
    harmonious influences:
The pulse of dew upon the grass kept his
    within its number,
And silent shadows from the trees refreshed
    him like a slumber.

VII

Wild timid hares were drawn from woods
    to share his home-caresses,
Uplooking to his human eyes with sylvan
    tendernesses:

The very world, by God's constraint, from
    falsehood's ways removing,
Its women and its men became, beside him,
    true and loving.

VIII

And though, in blindness, he remained
    unconscious of that guiding,
And things provided came without the
    sweet sense of providing,
He testified this solemn truth, while frenzy
    desolated,
—Nor man nor nature satisfies whom only
    God created.

IX

Like a sick child that knoweth not his
    mother while she blesses
And drops upon his burning brow the
    coolness of her kisses—
That turns his fevered eyes around—"My
    mother! where's my mother?"—
As if such tender words and deeds could
    come from any other!—

X

The fever gone, with leaps of heart he sees
    her bending o'er him,
Her face all pale from watchful love, the
    unweary love she bore him!
Thus woke the poet from the dream his
    life's long fever gave him,
Beneath those deep pathetic Eyes which
    closed in death to save him.

XI

Thus? oh, not *thus!* no type of earth can
    image that awaking,
Wherein he scarcely heard the chant of
    seraphs, round him breaking,
Or felt the new immortal throb of soul
    from body parted,
But felt those eyes alone, and knew—"*My*
    Savior! *not* deserted!"

XII

Deserted! Who hath dreamt that when
    the cross in darkness rested,
Upon the Victim's hidden face no love was
    manifested?
What frantic hands outstretched have e'er
    the atoning drops averted?
What tears have washed them from the
    soul, that *one* should be deserted?

XIII

Deserted! God could separate from his
    own essence rather;
And Adam's sins *have* swept between the
    righteous Son and Father:
Yea, once, Immanuel's orphaned cry his
    universe hath shaken—
It went up single, echoless, "My God, I am
    forsaken!"

XIV

It went up from the Holy's lips amid his
    lost creation,
That, of the lost, no son should use those
    words of desolation!

That Earth's worst frenzies, marring
    hope, should mar not hope's fruition,
And I, on Cowper's grave, should see his
    rapture in a vision.

From

Poems of 1844

THE SOUL'S EXPRESSION

With stammering lips and insufficient sound
I strive and struggle to deliver right
That music of my nature, day and night
With dream and thought and feeling interwound,
And inly answering all the senses round
With octaves of a mystic depth and height
Which step out grandly to the infinite
From the dark edges of the sensual ground.
This song of soul I struggle to outbear
Through portals of the sense, sublime and whole,
And utter all myself into the air;
But if I did it—as the thunder-roll
Breaks its own cloud, my flesh would perish there,
Before that dread apocalypse of soul.

LADY GERALDINE'S COURTSHIP
A Romance of the Age

A poet writes to his friend.
Place—*A room in Wycombe Hall.*
Time—*Late in the evening.*

Dear my friend and fellow student,
    I would lean my spirit o'er you!
Down the purple of this chamber, tears
    should scarcely run at will.
I am humbled who was humble. Friend,
    —I bow my head before you.
You should lead me to my peasants—
    but their faces are too still.

There's a lady—an earl's daughter—
    she is proud and she is noble,
And she treads the crimson carpet, and
    she breathes the perfumed air,
And a kingly blood sends glances up her
    princely eye to trouble,
And the shadow of a monarch's crown
    is softened in her hair.

She has halls among the woodlands,
    she has castles by the breakers,
She has farms and she has manors, she
    can threaten and command,
And the palpitating engines snort in
    steam across her acres,
As they mark upon the blasted heaven
    the measure of the land.

There are none of England's daughters
    who can show a prouder presence;
Upon princely suitors praying, she has
    looked in her disdain.
She was sprung of English nobles,
    I was born of English peasants;
What was *I* that I should love her—
    save for competence to pain?

I was only a poor poet, made for singing
    at her casement,
As the finches or the thrushes, while
    she thought of other things.
Oh, she walked so high above me, she
    appeared to my abasement,
In her lovely silken murmur, like an
    angel clad in wings!

Many vassals bow before her as her
    carriage sweeps their doorways;
She has blest their little children—as a
    priest or queen were she.
Far too tender, or too cruel far, her
    smile upon the poor was,
For I thought it was the same smile
    which she used to smile on *me*.

She has voters in the Commons, she has
    lovers in the palace;
And of all the fair court ladies, few have
    jewels half as fine;
Oft the prince has named her beauty
    'twixt the red wine and the chalice.
Oh, and what was *I* to love her? my
    beloved, my Geraldine!

Yet I could not choose but love her.
  I was born to poet-uses,
To love all things set above me, all of
  good and all of fair:
Nymphs of mountain, not of valley, we
  are wont to call the Muses
And in nympholeptic climbing, poets
  pass from mount to star.

And because I was a poet, and because
  the public praised me,
With a critical deduction for the modern
  writer's fault,
I could sit at rich men's tables—though
  the courtesìes that raised me,
Still suggested clear between us the
  pale spectrum of the salt.

And they praised me in her presence;
  —"Will your book appear this summer?"
Then returning to each other—"Yes,
  our plans are for the moors."
Then with whisper dropped behind me
  —"There he is! the latest comer!
Oh, she only likes his verses! what is
  over, she endures.

"Quite lowborn! self-educated! somewhat
  gifted though by nature—
And we make a point of asking him—
  of being very kind.
You may speak, he does not hear you!
  and besides, he writes no satire—
All those serpents kept by charmers
  leave the natural sting behind."

I grew scornfuller, grew colder, as I
          stood up there among them,
,   Till as frost intense will burn you, the
          cold scorning scorched my brow;
When a sudden silver speaking, gravely
          cadenced, over-rung them,
And a sudden silken stirring touched
          my inner nature through.

I looked upward and beheld her. With
          a calm and regnant spirit,
Slowly round she swept her eyelids,
          and said clear before them all—
"Have you such superfluous honor, sir,
          that able to confer it
You will come down, Mister Bertram,
          as my guest to Wycombe Hall?"

Here she paused—she had been paler
          at the first word of her speaking,
But because a silence followed it,
          blushed somewhat, as for shame,
Then, as scorning her own feeling,
          resumed calmly—"I am seeking
More distinction than these gentlemen
          think worthy of my claim.

"Ne'ertheless, you see, I seek it—not
          because I am a woman"
(Here her smile sprang like a fountain,
          and, so, overflowed her mouth),
"But because my woods in Sussex have
          some purple shades at gloaming
Which are worthy of a king in state, or
          poet in his youth.

"I invite you, Mister Bertram, to no
     scene for worldly speeches—
Sir, I scarce should dare—but only where
     God asked the thrushes first—
And if *you* will sing beside them, in the
     covert of my beeches,
I will thank you for the woodlands . . .
     for the human world, at worst."

Then she smiled around right childly,
     then she gazed around right queenly,
And I bowed—I could not answer;
     alternated light and gloom—
While as one who quells the lions, with
     a steady eye serenely,
She, with level fronting eyelids, passed
     out stately from the room.

Oh, the blessèd woods of Sussex, I can
     hear them still around me,
With their leafy tide of greenery still
     rippling up the wind.
Oh, the cursèd woods of Sussex! where
     the hunter's arrow found me,
When a fair face and a tender voice had
     made me mad and blind!

In that ancient hall of Wycombe, thronged
     the numerous guests invited,
And the lovely London ladies trod the
     floors with gliding feet;
And their voices low with fashion, not
     with feeling, softly freighted
All the air about the windows, with
     elastic laughters sweet.

For at eve, the open windows flung their
    light out on the terrace,
Which the floating orbs of curtains did
    with gradual shadow sweep,
While the swans upon the river, fed at
    morning by the heiress,
Trembled downward through their
    snowy wings at music in their sleep.

And there evermore was music, both of
    instrument and singing,
Till the finches of the shrubberies grew
    restless in the dark;
But the cedars stood up motionless,
    each in a moonlight ringing,
And the deer, half in the glimmer,
    strewed the hollows of the park.

And though sometimes she would bind me
    with her silver-corded speeches
To commix my words and laughter with
    the converse and the jest,
Oft I sate apart, and gazing on the river
    through the beeches,
Heard, as pure the swans swam down
    it, her pure voice o'erfloat the rest.

In the morning, horn of huntsman, hoof
    of steed, and laugh of rider,
Spread out cheery from the courtyard
    till we lost them in the hills,
While herself and other ladies, and her
    suitors left beside her,
Went a-wandering up the gardens
    through the laurels and abeles.

Thus, her foot upon the new-mown grass,
    bareheaded, with the flowing
Of the virginal white vesture gathered
    closely to her throat—
And the golden ringlets in her neck
    just quickened by her going,
And appearing to breathe sun for air,
    and doubting if to float—

With a branch of dewy maple, which
    her right hand held above her,
And which trembled a green shadow
    betwixt her and the skies,
As she turned her face in going, thus,
    she drew me on to love her,
And to worship the divineness of the
    smile hid in her eyes.

For her eyes alone smile constantly:
    her lips have serious sweetness,
And her front is calm—the dimple rarely
    ripples on the cheek;
But her deep blue eyes smile constantly,
    as if they in discreetness
Kept the secret of a happy dream she
    did not care to speak.

Thus she drew me the first morning,
    out across into the garden,
And I walked among her noble friends
    and could not keep behind.
Spake she unto all and unto me—
    "Behold, I am the warden
Of the songbirds in these lindens,
    which are cages to their mind.

"But within this swarded circle, into
    which the lime-walk brings us,
Whence the beeches, rounded greenly,
    stand away in reverent fear,
I will let no music enter, saving what
    the fountain sings us,
Which the lilies round the basin may
    seem pure enough to hear.

"The live air that waves the lilies waves
    the slender jet of water
Like a holy thought sent feebly up from
    soul of fasting saint:
Whereby lies a marble Silence, sleeping!
    (Lough the sculptor wrought her)
So asleep she is forgetting to say Hush!
    —a fancy quaint.

"Mark how heavy white her eyelids!
    not a dream between them lingers,
And the left hand's index droppeth from
    the lips upon the cheek;
While the right hand—with the symbol
    rose held slack within the fingers—
Has fallen backward in the basin—yet
    this Silence will not speak!

"That the essential meaning growing
    may exceed the special symbol,
Is the thought as I conceive it: it applies
    more high and low.
Our true noblemen will often through
    right nobleness grow humble,
And assert an inward honor by
    denying outward show."

"Nay, your Silence," said I, "truly, holds
    her symbol rose but slackly,
Yet *she holds it*—or would scarcely be a
    Silence to our ken;
And your nobles wear their ermine on
    the outside, or walk blackly
In the presence of the social law as
    mere ignoble men.

"Let the poets dream such dreaming!
    madam, in these British islands
'Tis the substance that wanes ever, 'tis
    the symbol that exceeds.
Soon we shall have naught but symbol!
    and, for statues like this Silence,
Shall accept the rose's image—in another
    case, the weed's."

"Not so quickly," she retorted—"I confess,
    where'er you go, you
Find for things, names—shows for
    actions, and pure gold for honor clear;
But when all is run to symbol in the
    Social, I will throw you
The world's book which now reads dryly
    and sit down with Silence here."

Half in playfulness she spoke, I thought,
    and half in indignation;
Friends who listened, laughed her words
    off, while her lovers deemed her fair:
A fair woman, flushed with feeling, in
    her noble-lighted station
Near the statue's white reposing—and
    both bathed in sunny air!—

With the trees round, not so distant but
    you heard their vernal murmur,
And beheld in light and shadow the
    leaves in and outward move,
And the little fountain leaping toward
    the sun-heart to be warmer,
Then recoiling in a tremble from the
    too much light above.

'Tis a picture for remembrance. And
    thus, morning after morning,
Did I follow as she drew me by the
    spirit to her feet.
Why, her greyhound followed also!
    dogs—we both were dogs for scorning—
To be sent back when she pleased it and
    her path lay through the wheat.

And thus, morning after morning, spite
    of vows and spite of sorrow,
Did I follow at her drawing, while the
    weekdays passed along,
Just to feed the swans this noontide, or
    to see the fawns tomorrow,
Or to teach the hillside echo some
    sweet Tuscan in a song.

Aye, for sometimes on the hillside, while
    we sate down in the gowans,
With the forest green behind us, and
    its shadow cast before,
And the river running under, and across
    it from the rowans
A brown partridge whirring near us,
    till we felt the air it bore—

There, obedient to her praying, did I
    read aloud the poems
Made to Tuscan flutes, or instruments
    more various of our own;
Read the pastoral parts of Spenser—or
    the subtle interflowings
Found in Petrarch's sonnets—here's the
    book—the leaf is folded down!

Or at times a modern volume—Wordsworth's
    solemn-thoughted idyll,
Howitt's ballad-verse, or Tennyson's
    enchanted reverie—
Or from Browning some "Pomegranate,"
    which, if cut deep down the middle,
Shows a heart within blood-tinctured,
    of a veined humanity.

Or at times I read there, hoarsely, some
    new poem of my making:
Poets ever fail in reading their own
    verses to their worth—
For the echo in you breaks upon the
    words which you are speaking,
And the chariot wheels jar in the gate
    through which you drive them forth.

After, when we were grown tired of
    books, the silence round us flinging
A slow arm of sweet compression, felt
    with beatings at the breast,
She would break out, on a sudden, in
    a gush of woodland singing,
Like a child's emotion in a god—a naiad
    tired of rest.

Oh, to see or hear her singing! scarce
    I know which is divinest—
For her looks sing too—she modulates
    her gestures on the tune;
And her mouth stirs with the song, like
    song; and when the notes are finest,
'Tis the eyes that shoot out vocal light
    and seem to swell them on.

Then we talked—oh, how we talked! her
    voice, so cadenced in the talking,
Made another singing—of the soul!
    a music without bars;
While the leafy sounds of woodlands,
    humming round where we were walking,
Brought interposition worthy-sweet—
    as skies about the stars.

And she spake such good thoughts
    natural, as if she always thought them;
She had sympathies so rapid, open, free
    as bird on branch,
Just as ready to fly east as west, whichever
    way besought them,
In the birchen-wood a chirrup, or a
    cock-crow in the grange.

In her utmost lightness there is truth—
    and often she speaks lightly,
Has a grace in being gay, which even
    mournful souls approve,
For the root of some grave earnest
    thought is understruck so rightly
As to justify the foliage and the waving
    flowers above.

And she talked on—*we* talked, rather!
    upon all things, substance, shadow,
Of the sheep that browsed the grasses,
    of the reapers in the corn,
Of the little children from the schools,
    seen winding through the meadow—
Of the poor rich world beyond them, still
    kept poorer by its scorn.

So, of men, and so, of letters—books are
    men of higher stature,
And the only men that speak aloud for
    future times to hear;
So, of mankind in the abstract, which
    grows slowly into nature,
Yet will lift the cry of "progress," as it
    trod from sphere to sphere.

And her custom was to praise me when
    I said—"The Age culls simples,
With a broad clown's back turned
    broadly to the glory of the stars.
We are gods by our own reck'ning, and
    may well shut up the temples,
And wield on, amid the incense-steam,
    the thunder of our cars.

"For we throw out acclamations of
    self-thanking, self-admiring,
With, at every mile run faster—'O the
    wondrous wondrous age,'
Little thinking if we work our SOULS as
    nobly as our iron,
Or if angels will commend us at the goal
    of pilgrimage.

"Why, what *is* this patient entrance
    into nature's deep resources,
But the child's most gradual learning to
    walk upright without bane?
When we drive out, from the cloud of
    steam, majestical white horses,
Are we greater than the first men who
    led black ones by the mane?

"If we trod the deeps of ocean, if we
    struck the stars in rising,
If we wrapped the globe intensely with
    one hot electric breath,
'Twere but power within our tether, no
    new spirit-power comprising,
And in life we were not greater men,
    nor bolder men in death."

She was patient with my talking; and
    I loved her, loved her, certes,
As I loved all heavenly objects, with
    uplifted eyes and hands!
As I loved pure inspirations, loved the
    graces, loved the virtues,
In a Love content with writing his own
    name on desert sands.

Or at least I thought so, purely!—thought
    no idiot Hope was raising
Any crown to crown Love's silence—
    silent Love that sate alone.
Out, alas! the stag is like me—he, that
    tries to go on grazing
With the great deep gun-wound in his
    neck, then reels with sudden moan.

It was thus I reeled. I told you that her
    hand had many suitors;
But she smiles them down imperially,
    as Venus did the waves,
And with such a gracious coldness, that
    they cannot press their futures
On the present of her courtesy, which
    yieldingly enslaves.

And this morning, as I sate alone within
    the inner chamber,
With the great saloon beyond it, lost in
    pleasant thought serene,
For I had been reading Camöens—that
    poem you remember,
Which his lady's eyes are praised in, as
    the sweetest ever seen.

And the book lay open, and my thought
    flew from it, taking from it
A vibration and impulsion to an end
    beyond its own,
As the branch of a green osier, when a
    child would overcome it,
Springs up freely from his clasping and
    goes swinging in the sun.

As I mused I heard a murmur—it grew
    deep as it grew longer—
Speakers using earnest language—
    "Lady Geraldine, you *would!*"
And I heard a voice that pleaded ever
    on, in accents stronger
As a sense of reason gave it power to
    make its rhetoric good.

Well I knew that voice—it was an earl's,
    of soul that matched his station,
Soul completed into lordship—might and
    right read on his brow;
Very finely courteous—far too proud to
    doubt his domination
Of the common people, he atones for
    grandeur by a bow.

High straight forehead, nose of eagle,
    cold blue eyes, of less expression
Than resistance, coldly casting off the
    looks of other men,
As steel, arrows—unelastic lips, which
    seem to taste possession,
And be cautious lest the common air
    should injure or distrain.

For the rest, accomplished, upright—
    aye, and standing by his order
With a bearing not ungraceful; fond of
    art and letters too;
Just a good man made a proud man—as
    the sandy rocks that border
A wild coast, by circumstances, in a
    regnant ebb and flow.

Thus, I knew that voice—I heard it, and
    I could not help the hearkening.
In the room I stood up blindly, and my
    burning heart within
Seemed to seethe and fuse my senses, till
    they ran on all sides darkening,
And scorched, weighed, like melted metal
    round my feet that stood therein.

And that voice, I heard it pleading, for
 love's sake, for wealth, position,
For the sake of liberal uses, and great
 actions to be done—
And she interrupted gently, "Nay, my
 lord, the old tradition
Of your Normans, by some worthier hand
 than mine is, should be won."

"Ah, that white hand!" he said quickly—
 and in his he either drew it
Or attempted—for with gravity and
 instance she replied,
"Nay, indeed, my lord, this talk is vain,
 and we had best eschew it,
And pass on, like friends, to other points
 less easy to decide."

What he said again, I know not. It is
 likely that his trouble
Worked his pride up to the surface, for
 she answered in slow scorn,
"And your lordship judges rightly.
 Whom I marry, shall be noble,
Aye, and wealthy. I shall never blush
 to think how he was born."

There, I maddened! her words stung me.
 Life swept through me into fever,
And my soul sprang up astonished,
 sprang, full-statured in an hour.
Know you what it is when anguish, with
 apocalyptic NEVER,
To a Pythian height dilates you—and
 despair sublimes to power?

From my brain, the soul-wings budded—
    waved a flame about my body,
Whence conventions coiled to ashes,
    I felt self-drawn out, as man,
From amalgamate false natures, and I
    saw the skies grow ruddy
With the deepening feet of angels, and
    I knew what spirits can.

I was mad—inspired—say either!
    (anguish worketh inspiration)
Was a man, or beast—perhaps so, for
    the tiger roars, when speared;
And I walked on, step by step, along
    the level of my passion—
Oh my soul! and passed the doorway
    to her face, and never feared.

He had left her, peradventure, when my
    footstep proved my coming—
But for *her*—she half arose, then sate—
    grew scarlet and grew pale.
Oh, she trembled!—'tis so always with
    a worldly man or woman
In the presence of true spirits—what else
    can they do but quail?

Oh, she fluttered like a tame bird, in
    among its forest-brothers
Far too strong for it; then drooping,
    bowed her face upon her hands—
And I spake out wildly, fiercely, brutal
    truths of her and others:
I, she planted in the desert, swathed her,
    windlike, with my sands.

I plucked up her social fictions,
 bloody-rooted though leaf-verdant—
Trod them down with words of shaming,
 —all the purple and the gold,
All the "landed stakes" and lordships,
 all, that spirits pure and ardent
Are cast out of love and honor because
 chancing not to hold.

"For myself I do not argue," said I,
 "though I love you, madam,
But for better souls that nearer to the
 height of yours have trod;
And this age shows, to my thinking, still
 more infidels to Adam,
Than directly, by profession, simple
 infidels to God.

"Yet, O God," I said, "O grave," I said,
 "O mother's heart and bosom,
With whom first and last are equal,
 saint and corpse and little child!
We are fools to your deductions, in these
 figments of heart-closing;
We are traitors to your causes, in these
 sympathies defiled.

"Learn more reverence, madam, not for
 rank or wealth—*that* needs no learning,
That comes quickly—quick as sin does,
 aye, and culminates to sin;
But for Adam's seed, MAN! Trust me,
 'tis a clay above your scorning,
With God's image stamped upon it, and
 God's kindling breath within.

"What right have you, madam, gazing in
        your palace mirror daily,
Getting so by heart your beauty which
        all others must adore,
While you draw the golden ringlets down
        your fingers, to vow gaily
You will wed no man that's only good to
        God, and nothing more?

"Why, what right have you, made fair
        by that same God—the sweetest woman
Of all women He has fashioned—with
        your lovely spirit-face,
Which would seem too near to vanish if
        its smile were not so human,
And your voice of holy sweetness, turning
        common words to grace,

"What right *can* you have, God's other
        works to scorn, despise, revile them
In the gross, as mere men, broadly—not
        as *noble* men, forsooth—
As mere Parias of the outer world,
        forbidden to assoil them
In the hope of living, dying, near that
        sweetness of your mouth?

"Have you any answer, madam? If my
        spirit were less earthly,
If its instrument were gifted with a better
        silver string,
I would kneel down where I stand, and
        say—Behold me! I am worthy
Of thy loving, for I love thee! I am
        worthy as a king.

— 47 —

"As it is—your ermined pride, I swear,
    shall feel this stain upon her,
That *I*, poor, weak, tossed with passion,
    scorned by me and you again,
Love you, madam—dare to love you—to
    my grief and your dishonor,
To my endless desolation, and your
    impotent disdain!"

More mad words like these—mere madness!
    friend, I need not write them fuller,
For I hear my hot soul dropping on the
    lines in showers of tears.
Oh, a woman! friend, a woman! why,
    a beast had scarce been duller
Than roar bestial loud complaints against
    the shining of the spheres.

But at last there came a pause. I stood
    all vibrating with thunder
Which my soul had used. The silence
    drew her face up like a call.
Could you guess what word she uttered?
    She looked up, as if in wonder,
With tears beaded on her lashes, and
    said "Bertram!"—it was all.

If she had cursed me, and she might have
    —of if even, with queenly bearing
Which at need is used by women, she
    had risen up and said,
"Sir, you are my guest, and therefore I
    have given you a full hearing,
Now, beseech you, choose a name exacting
    somewhat less, instead,"—

I had borne it!—but that "Bertram"—
  why it lies there on the paper
A mere word, without her accent—and
  you cannot judge the weight
Of the calm which crushed my passion:
  I seemed drowning in a vapor—
And her gentleness destroyed me whom
  her scorn made desolate.

So, struck backward and exhausted by
  that inward flow of passion
Which had rushed on, sparing nothing,
  into forms of abstract truth,
By a logic agonizing through unseemly
  demonstration,
And by youth's own anguish turning
  grimly gray the hairs of youth—

By the sense accursed and instant, that
  if even I spake wisely
I spake basely—using truth, if what I
  spake, indeed was true,
To avenge wrong on a woman—*her,* who
  sate there weighing nicely
A poor manhood's worth, found guilty of
  such deeds as I could do!—

By such wrong and woe exhausted—
  what I suffered and occasioned—
As a wild horse through a city runs with
  lightning in his eyes,
And then dashing at a church's cold and
  passive wall, impassioned,
Strikes the death into his burning brain,
  and blindly drops and dies—

So I fell, struck down before her! do
    you blame me, friend, for weakness?
'Twas my strength of passion slew me!
    —fell before her like a stone.
Fast the dreadful world rolled from me,
    on its roaring wheels of blackness—
When the light came, I was lying in this
    chamber, and alone.

Oh, of course, she charged her lackeys
    to bear out the sickly burden,
And to cast it from her scornful sight—
    but not *beyond* the gate;
She is too kind to be cruel, and too
    haughty not to pardon
Such a man as I—'twere something to
    be level to her hate.

But for me—you now are conscious
    why, my friend, I write this letter,
How my life is read all backward, and
    the charm of life undone:
I shall leave her house at dawn; I would
    tonight, if I were better—
And I charge my soul to hold my body
    strengthened for the sun.

When the sun has dyed the oriel, I depart,
    with no last gazes,
No weak moanings (one word only, left
    in writing for her hands),
Out of reach of all derision, and some
    unavailing praises,
To make front against this anguish in the
    far and foreign lands.

Blame me not. I would not squander
    life in grief—I am abstemious:
I but nurse my spirit's falcon, that its
    wing may soar again.
There's no room for tears of weakness in
    the blind eyes of a Phemius!
Into work the poet kneads them—and
    he does not die *till then*.

CONCLUSION

Bertram finished the last pages, while
    along the silence ever
Still in hot and heavy splashes, fell the
    tears on every leaf:
Having ended he leans backward in his
    chair, with lips that quiver
From the deep unspoken, aye, and deep
    unwritten thoughts of grief.

Soh! how still the lady standeth! 'tis a
    dream—a dream of mercies!
'Twixt the purple lattice curtains, how
    she standeth still and pale!
'Tis a vision, sure, of mercies, sent to
    soften his self-curses—
Sent to sweep a patient quiet o'er the
    tossing of his wail.

"Eyes," he said, "now throbbing through
    me! are ye eyes that did undo me?
Shining eyes, like antique jewels set in
    Parian statue-stone!
Underneath that calm white forehead, are
    ye ever burning torrid
O'er the desolate sand-desert of my heart
    and life undone?"

With a murmurous stir uncertain, in the
    air, the purple curtain
Swelleth in and swelleth out around her
    motionless pale brows,
While the gliding of the river sends a
    rippling noise forever
Through the open casement whitened by
    the moonlight's slant repose.

Said he—"Vision of a lady! stand there
    silent, stand there steady!
Now I see it plainly, plainly; now I
    cannot hope or doubt—
There, the brows of mild repression—
    there, the lips of silent passion,
Curvèd like an archer's bow to send the
    bitter arrows out."

Ever, evermore the while in a slow
    silence she kept smiling,
And approached him slowly, slowly, in
    a gliding measured pace;
With her two white hands extended, as
    if praying one offended,
And a look of supplication, gazing earnest
    in his face.

Said he—"Wake me by no gesture—
    sound of breath, or stir of vesture!
Let the blessèd apparition melt not yet
    to its divine!
No approaching—hush, no breathing! or
    my heart must swoon to death in
The too utter life thou bringest—O thou
    dream of Geraldine!"

Ever, evermore the while in a slow
  silence she kept smiling—
But the tears ran over lightly from her
  eyes, and tenderly;
"Dost thou, Bertram, truly love me?
  Is no woman far above me
Found more worthy of thy poet-heart
  than such a one as *I*?"

Said he—"I would dream so ever, like
  the flowing of that river,
Flowing ever in a shadow greenly onward
  to the sea!
So, thou vision of all sweetness—princely
  to a full completeness—
Would my heart and life flow onward—
  deathward—through this dream of THEE!"

Ever, evermore the while in a slow
  silence she kept smiling,
While the silver tears ran faster down
  the blushing of her cheeks;
Then with both her hands enfolding both
  of his, she softly told him,
"Bertram, if I say I love thee . . . 'tis
  the vision only speaks."

Softened, quickened to adore her, on his
  knee be fell before her—
And she whispered low in triumph, "It
  shall be as I have sworn!
Very rich he is in virtues—very noble—
  noble, certes;
And I shall not blush in knowing that
  men call him lowly born."

THE LADY'S YES

I

"Yes," I answered you last night;
  "No," this morning, sir, I say.
Colors seen by candlelight
  Will not look the same by day.

II

When the viols played their best,
  Lamps above and laughs below,
Love me sounded like a jest,
  Fit for *yes* or fit for *no*.

III

Call me false or call me free—
  Vow, whatever light may shine,
No man on your face shall see
  Any grief for change on mine.

IV

Yet the sin is on us both;
  Time to dance is not to woo;
Wooing light makes fickle troth,
  Scorn of *me* recoils on *you*.

V

Learn to win a lady's faith
  Nobly as the thing is high,
Bravely, as for life and death—
  With a loyal gravity.

VI

Lead her from the festive boards,
　　Point her to the starry skies;
Guard her, by your truthful words,
　　Pure from courtship's flatteries.

VII

By your truth she shall be true,
　　Ever true, as wives of yore,
And her yes, once said to you,
　　SHALL be Yes forevermore.

THE LOST BOWER

I

In the pleasant orchard closes,
"God bless all our gains," say we;
But "May God bless all our losses,"
Better suits with our degree.
Listen, gentle—ay, and simple! listen, children on the
knee!

II

Green the land is where my daily
Steps in jocund childhood played,
Dimpled close with hill and valley,
Dappled very close with shade;
Summer-snow of apple blossoms running up from glade to
glade.

III

There is one hill I see nearer,
In my vision of the rest;
And a little wood seems clearer
As it climbeth from the west,
Sideway from the tree-locked valley, to the airy upland
crest.

IV

Small the wood is, green with hazels,
And, completing the ascent,
Where the wind blows and sun dazzles
Thrills in leafy tremblement,
Like a heart that after climbing beateth quickly through
content.

V

Not a step the wood advances
O'er the open hilltops bound;
There, in green arrest, the branches
See their image on the ground:
You may walk beneath them smiling, glad with sight and
glad with sound.

VI

For you harken on your right hand,
How the birds do leap and call
In the greenwood, out of sight and
Out of reach and fear of all;
And the squirrels crack the filberts through their cheerful
madrigal.

VII

On your left, the sheep are cropping
The slant grass and daisies pale,
And five apple trees stand dropping
Separate shadows toward the vale
Over which, in choral silence, the hills look you their "All
hail!"

VIII

Far out, kindled by each other,
Shining hills on hills arise,
Close as brother leans to brother
When they press beneath the eyes
Of some father praying blessings from the gifts of paradise.

IX

While beyond, above them mounted,
And above their woods alsò,
Malvern hills, for mountains counted

Not unduly, loom a-row—
Keepers of Piers Plowman's visions through the sunshine
and the snow.

X

Yet, in childhood, little prized I
That fair walk and far survey;
'Twas a straight walk unadvised by
The least mischief worth a nay;
Up and down—as dull as grammar on the eve of
holiday.

XI

But the wood, all close and clenching
Bough in bough and root in root—
No more sky (for over-branching)
At your head than at your foot—
Oh, the wood drew me within it by a glamour past
dispute!

XII

Few and broken paths showed through it,
Where the sheep had tried to run—
Forced with snowy wool to strew it
Round the thickets, when anon
They, with silly thorn-pricked noses, bleated back into
the sun.

XIII

But my childish heart beat stronger
Than those thickets dared to grow:
I could pierce them! *I* could longer
Travel on, methought, than so:
Sheep for sheep-paths! braver children climb and creep
where they would go.

XIV

And the poets wander, (said I,)
Over places all as rude:
Bold Rinaldo's lovely lady
Sate to meet him in a wood:
Rosalinda, like a fountain, laughed out pure with solitude.

XV

And if Chaucer had not traveled
Through a forest by a well,
He had never dreamt nor marveled
At those ladies fair and fell
Who lived smiling without loving in their island-citadel.

XVI

Thus I thought of the old singers
And took courage from their song,
Till my little struggling fingers
Tore asunder gyve and thong
Of the brambles which entrapped me, and the barrier
        branches strong.

XVII

On a day, such pastime keeping,
With a fawn's heart debonair,
Under-crawling, overleaping
Thorns that prick and boughs that bear,
I stood suddenly astonied—I was gladdened unaware.

XVIII

From the place I stood in, floated
Back the covert dim and close,
Anti the open ground was coated
Carpet-smooth with grass and moss,
And the bluebell's purple presence signed it worthily
        across.

XIX

Here a linden tree stood, bright'ning
All adown its silver rind;
For as some trees draw the lightning,
So this tree, unto my mind,
Drew to earth the blessed sunshine from the sky where
it was shrined.

XX

Tall the linden tree and near it
An old hawthorn also grew;
And wood-ivy like a spirit
Hovered dimly round the two,
Shaping thence that bower of beauty which I sing of thus
to you.

XXI

'Twas a bower for garden fitter
Than for any woodland wide:
Though a fresh and dewy glitter
Struck it through from side to side,
Shaped and shaven was the freshness, as by garden-cunning
plied.

XXII

Oh, a lady might have come there,
Hooded fairly like her hawk,
With a book or lute in summer,
And a hope of sweeter talk—
Listening less to her own music than for footsteps on
the walk.

XXIII

But that bower appeared a marvel
In the wildness of the place;
With such seeming art and travail,

Finely fixed and fitted was
Leaf to leaf, the dark-green ivy, to the summit from the base.

XXIV

And the ivy veined and glossy
Was enwrought with eglantine;
And the wild hop fibered closely,
And the large-leaved columbine,
Arch of door and window-mullion, did right sylvanly
    entwine.

XXV

Rose trees either side the door were
Growing lithe and growing tall,
Each one set, a summer warder
For the keeping of the hall—
With a red rose and a white rose, leaning, nodding at the
    wall.

XXVI

As I entered, mosses hushing
Stole all noises from my foot;
And a green elastic cushion,
Clasped within the linden's root,
Took me in a chair of silence very rare and absolute.

XXVII

All the floor was paved with glory,
Greenly, silently inlaid
(Through quick motions made before me)
With fair counterparts in shade
Of the fair serrated ivy-leaves which slanted overhead.

XXVIII

"Is such pavement in a palace?"
So I questioned in my thought:

The sun, shining through the chalice
Of the red rose hung without,
Threw within a red libation, like an answer to my doubt.

XXIX

At the same time, on the linen
Of my childish lap there fell
Two white may-leaves, downward winning
Through the ceiling's miracle,
From a blossom, like an angel, out of sight yet blessing
well.

XXX

Down to floor and up to ceiling
Quick I turned my childish face,
With an innocent appealing
For the secret of the place
To the trees, which surely knew it in partaking of the
grace.

XXXI

Where's no foot of human creature
How could reach a human hand?
And if this be work of nature,
Why has nature turned so bland,
Breaking off from other wild-work? It was hard to
understand.

XXXII

Was she weary of rough-doing,
Of the bramble and the thorn?
Did she pause in tender rueing
Here of all her sylvan scorn?
Or in mock of art's deceiving was the sudden mildness
worn?

— 62 —

XXXIII

Or could this same bower (I fancied)
Be the work of Dryad strong,
Who, surviving all that chancëd
In the world's old pagan wrong,
Lay hid, feeding in the woodland on the last true poet's song?

XXXIV

Or was this the house of fairies,
Left, because of the rough ways,
Unassoiled by Ave Marys
Which the passing pilgrim prays,
And beyond St. Catherine's chiming on the blessed
      Sabbath days?

XXXV

So, young mouser, I sate listening
To my fancy's wildest word.
On a sudden, through the glistening
Leaves around, a little stirred,
Came a sound, a sense of music which was rather felt
      than heard.

XXXVI

Softly, finely, it enwound me;
From the world it shut me in—
Like a fountain falling round me,
Which with silver waters thin
Clips a little water Naiad sitting smilingly within.

XXXVII

Whence the music came, who knoweth?
I know nothing: but indeed
Pan or Faunus never bloweth
So much sweetness from a reed
Which has sucked the milk of waters at the oldest riverhead.

XXXVIII

Never lark the sun can waken
With such sweetness! when the lark,
The high planets overtaking
In the half-evanished Dark,
Casts his singing to their singing, like an arrow to the
    mark.

XXXIX

Never nightingale so singeth:
Oh, she leans on thorny tree
And her poet-song she flingeth
Over pain to victory!
Yet she never sings such music—or she sings it not to me.

XL

Never blackbirds, never thrushes
Nor small finches sing so sweet,
When the sun strikes through the bushes
To their crimson clinging feet,
And their pretty eyes look sideways to the summer heavens
    complete.

XLI

If it *were* a bird, it seemëd
Most like Chaucer's, which, in sooth,
He of green and azure dreamèd,
While it sate in spirit-ruth
On that bier of a crowned lady, singing nigh her silent
    mouth.

XLII

If it *were* a bird?—ah, skeptic,
Give me "yea" or give me "nay"—
Though my soul were nympholeptic

As I heard that virëlay,
You may stoop your pride to pardon, for my sin is far
away!

XLIII

I rose up in exaltation
And an inward trembling heat,
And (it seemed) in geste of passion
Dropped the music to my feet
Like a garment rustling downwards—such a silence
followed it!

XLIV

Heart and head beat through the quiet
Full and heavily, though slower:
In the song, I think, and by it,
Mystic Presences of power
Had up-snatched me to the Timeless, then returned
me to the Hour.

XLV

In a child-abstraction lifted,
Straightway from the bower I passed,
Foot and soul being dimly drifted
Through the greenwood, till, at last,
In the hilltop's open sunshine I all consciously was
cast.

XLVI

Face to face with the true mountains
I stood silently and still,
Drawing strength from fancy's dauntings,
From the air about the hill
And from Nature's open mercies and most debonair
goodwill.

— 65 —

Oh, the golden-hearted daisies
Witnessed there, before my youth,
To the truth of things, with praises
Of the beauty of the truth;
And I woke to Nature's real, laughing joyfully for both.

And I said within me, laughing,
"I have found a bower today,
A green lusus, fashioned half in
Chance and half in Nature's play;
And a little bird sings nigh it, I will nevermore missay.

"Henceforth, *I* will be the fairy
Of this bower not built by one;
I will go there, sad or merry,
With each morning's benison,
And the bird shall be my harper in the dream-hall I have
    won."

So I said. But the next morning,
(—Child, look up into my face—
'Ware, oh skeptic, of your scorning!
This is truth in its pure grace!)
The next morning all had vanished, or my wandering
    missed the place.

Bring an oath most sylvan-holy,
And upon it swear me true—
By the wind-bells swinging slowly
Their mute curfews in the dew,
By the advent of the snowdrop, by the rosemary and rue—

I affirm by all or any,
Let the cause be charm or chance,
That my wandering searches many
Missed the bower of my romance—
That I nevermore upon it turned my mortal countenance.

LIII

I affirm that, since I lost it,
Never bower has seemed so fair;
Never garden-creeper crossed it
With so deft and brave an air,
Never bird sung in the summer, as I saw and heard them there.

LIV

Day by day, with new desire,
Toward my wood I ran in faith,
Under leaf and over brier,
Through the thickets, out of breath;
Like the prince who rescued Beauty from the sleep as long
    as death.

LV

But his sword of mettle clashëd,
And his arm smote strong, I ween,
And her dreaming spirit flashëd
Through her body's fair white screen,
And the light thereof might guide him up the cedar alleys
    green:

LVI

But for me I saw no splendor—
All my sword was my child-heart;
And the wood refused surrender
Of that bower it held apart,
Safe as Oedipus's grave-place 'mid Colone's olives swart.

LVII

As Aladdin sought the basements
His fair palace rose upon,
And the four-and-twenty casements
Which gave answers to the sun;
So, in wilderment of gazing, I looked up and I looked down.

LVIII

Years have vanished since, as wholly
As the little bower did then;
And you call it tender folly
That such thoughts should come again?
Ah, I cannot change this sighing for your smiling, brother
     men!

LIX

For this loss it did prefigure
Other loss of better good,
When my soul, in spirit vigor
And in ripened womanhood,
Fell from visions of more beauty than an arbor in a wood.

LX

I have lost—oh, many a pleasure,
Many a hope and many a power—
Studious health and merry leisure,
The first dew on the first flower!
But the first of all my losses was the losing of the bower.

LXI

I have lost the dream of Doing,
And the other dream of Done,
The first spring in the pursuing,
The first pride in the Begun—
First recoil from incompletion, in the face of what is
     won—

LXII

Exaltations in the far light
Where some cottage only is;
Mild dejections in the starlight,
Which the sadder-hearted miss;
And the child-cheek blushing scarlet for the very shame of
  bliss.

LXIII

I have lost the sound child-sleeping
Which the thunder could not break;
Something too of the strong leaping
Of the staglike heart awake,
Which the pale is low for keeping in the road it ought to take.

LXIV

Some respect to social fictions
Has been also lost by me;
And some generous genuflections,
Which my spirit offered free
To the pleasant old conventions of our false humanity.

LXV

All my losses did I tell you,
Ye perchance would look away—
Ye would answer me, "Farewell! you
Make sad company today,
And your tears are falling faster than the bitter words you
  say."

LXVI

For God placed me like a dial
In the open ground with power,
And my heart had for its trial
All the sun and all the shower:
And I suffered many losses—and my first was of the bower.

LXVII

Laugh you? If that loss of mine be
Of no heavy-seeming weight—
When the cone falls from the pine tree,
The young children laugh thereat;
Yet the wind that struck it, riseth, and the tempest shall be
    great.

LXVIII

One who knew me in my childhood
In the glamour and the game,
Looking on me long and mild, would
Never know me for the same.
Come, unchanging recollections, where those changes
    overcame!

LXIX

By this couch I weakly lie on,
While I count my memories—
Through the fingers which, still sighing,
I press closely on mine eyes—
Clear as once beneath the sunshine, I behold the bower arise.

LXX

Springs the linden tree as greenly,
Stroked with light adown its rind;
And the ivy-leaves serenely
Each in either intertwined;
And the rose trees at the doorway, they have neither grown
    nor pined.

LXXI

From those overblown faint roses
Not a leaf appeareth shed,
And that little bud discloses

Not a thorn's-breadth more of red
For the winters and the summers which have passed me
    overhead.

LXXII

And that music overfloweth,
Sudden sweet, the sylvan eaves:
Thrush or nightingale—who knoweth?
Fay or Faunus—who believes?
But my heart still trembles in me to the trembling of the
    leaves.

LXXIII

Is the bower lost, then? who sayeth
That the bower indeed is lost?
Hark! my spirit in it prayeth
Through the sunshine and the frost—
And the prayer preserves it greenly, to the last and uttermost.

LXXIV

Till another open for me
In God's Eden-land unknown,
With an angel at the doorway,
White with gazing at His throne;
And a saint's voice in the palm trees, singing—"All is lost . . .
    and won!"

THE CRY OF THE CHILDREN

I

Do ye hear the children weeping, O my brothers,
 Ere the sorrow comes with years?
They are leaning their young heads against their mothers,
 And *that* cannot stop their tears.
The young lambs are bleating in the meadows,
 The young birds are chirping in the nest,
The young fawns are playing with the shadows,
 The young flowers are blowing toward the west—
But the young, young children, O my brothers,
 They are weeping bitterly!
They are weeping in the playtime of the others,
 In the country of the free.

II

Do you question the young children in the sorrow
 Why their tears are falling so?
The old man may weep for his tomorrow
 Which is lost in Long Ago;
The old tree is leafless in the forest,
 The old year is ending in the frost,
The old wound, if stricken, is the sorest,
 The old hope is hardest to be lost.
But the young, young children, O my brothers,
 Do you ask them why they stand
Weeping sore before the bosoms of their mothers,
 In our happy Fatherland?

III

They look up with their pale and sunken faces,
 And their looks are sad to see,

For the man's hoary anguish draws and presses
    Down the cheeks of infancy.
"Your old earth," they say, "is very dreary;
    Our young feet," they say, "are very weak!
Few paces have we taken, yet are weary—
    Our grave-rest is very far to seek.
Ask the aged why they weep, and not the children;
    For the outside earth is cold;
And we young ones stand without, in our bewildering,
    And the graves are for the old."

IV

"True," say the children, "it may happen
    That we die before our time;
Little Alice died last year—her grave is shapen
    Like a snowball, in the rime.
We looked into the pit prepared to take her:
    Was no room for any work in the close clay!
From the sleep wherein she lieth none will wake her,
    Crying, 'Get up, little Alice! it is day.'
If you listen by that grave, in sun and shower,
    With your ear down, little Alice never cries;
Could we see her face, be sure we should not know her,
    For the smile has time for growing in her eyes:
And merry go her moments, luffed and stilled in
    The shroud by the kirk-chime.
It is good when it happens," say the children,
    "That we die before our time."

V

Alas, alas, the children! they are seeking
    Death in life, as best to have;
They are binding up their hearts away from breaking,
    With a cerement from the grave.
Go out, children, from the mine and from the city,

Sing out, children, as the little thrushes do;
Pluck you handfuls of the meadow-cowslips pretty,
   Laugh aloud, to feel your fingers let them through!
But they answer, "Are your cowslips of the meadows
     like our weeds anear the mine?
Leave us quiet in the dark of the coal-shadows,
    From your pleasures fair and fine!

VI

"For oh," say the children, "we are weary,
    And we cannot run or leap;
If we cared for any meadows, it were merely
    To drop down in them and sleep.
Our knees tremble sorely in the stooping,
    We fall upon our faces, trying to go;
And, underneath our heavy eyelids drooping,
    The reddest flower would look as pale as snow;
For, all day, we drag our burden tiring
    Through the coal-dark, underground—
Or, all day, we drive the wheels of iron
    In the factories, round and round.

VII

"For all day, the wheels are droning, turning;
    Their wind comes in our faces—
Till our hearts turn—our heads with pulses burning,
    And the walls turn in their places:
Turns the sky in the high window blank and reeling,
    Turns the long light that drops adown the wall,
Turn the black flies that crawl along the ceiling,
    All are turning, all the day, and we with all.
And all day, the iron wheels are droning,
    And sometimes we could pray,
'O ye wheels,' (breaking out in a mad moaning)
    'Stop! be silent for today!' "

VIII

Aye, be silent! Let them hear each other breathing
 For a moment, mouth to mouth!
Let them touch each other's hands, in a fresh wreathing
 Of their tender human youth!
Let them feel that this cold metallic motion
 Is not all the life God fashions or reveals:
Let them prove their living souls against the notion
 That they live in you, or under you, O wheels!—
Still, all day, the iron wheels go onward,
 Grinding life down from its mark;
And the children's souls, which God is calling sunward,
 Spin on blindly in the dark.

IX

Now tell the poor young children, O my brothers,
 To look up to Him and pray;
So the blessed One who blesseth all the others,
 Will bless them another day.
They answer, "Who is God that He should hear us,
 While the rushing of the iron wheels is stirred?
When we sob aloud, the human creatures near us
 Pass by, hearing not, or answer not a word.
And *we* hear not (for the wheels in their resounding)
 Strangers speaking at the door:
Is it likely God, with angels singing round him,
 Hears our weeping any more?

X

"Two words, indeed, of praying we remember,
 And at midnight's hour of harm,
'Our Father,' looking upward in the chamber,
 We say softly for a charm.
We know no other words except 'Our Father,'
 And we think that, in some pause of angels' song,

God may pluck them with the silence sweet to gather,
  And hold both within His right hand which is strong.
'Our Father!' If He heard us, He would surely
  (For they call Him good and mild)
Answer, smiling down the steep world very purely,
  'Come and rest with Me, My child.'"

XI

"But no!" say the children, weeping faster,
  "He is speechless as a stone:
And they tell us, of His image is the master
  Who commands us to work on.
Go to!" say the children—"up in heaven,
  Dark, wheel-like, turning clouds are all we find.
Do not mock us; grief has made us unbelieving—
  We look up for God, but tears have made us blind."
Do you hear the children weeping and disproving,
  O my brothers, what ye preach?
For God's possible is taught by His world's loving,
  And the children doubt of each.

XII

And well may the children weep before you!
  They are weary ere they run;
They have never seen the sunshine, nor the glory
  Which is brighter than the sun.
They know the grief of man, without its wisdom;
  They sink in man's despair, without its calm;
Are slaves, without the liberty in Christdom,
  Are martyrs, by the pang without the palm—
Are worn as if with age, yet unretrievingly
  The harvest of its memories cannot reap—
Are orphans of the earthly love and heavenly.
  Let them weep! let them weep!

XIII

They look up with their pale and sunken faces,
    And their look is dread to see,
For they mind you of their angels in high places,
    With eyes turned on Deity!—
"How long," they say, "how long, O cruel nation,
    Will you stand, to move the world, on a child's heart—
Stifle down with a mailed heel its palpitation,
    And tread onward to your throne amid the mart?
Our blood splashes upward, O gold-heaper,
    And your purple shows your path!
But the child's sob in the silence curses deeper
    Than the strong man in his wrath."

TO FLUSH, MY DOG

I

Loving friend, the gift of one
Who her own true faith has run
   Through my lower nature,
Be my benediction said
With hand upon thy head,
   Gentle fellow-creature!

II

Like a lady's ringlets brown,
Flow thy silken ears adown
   Either side demurely
Of thy silver-suited breast
Shining out from all the rest
   Of thy body purely.

III

Darkly brown thy body is,
Till the sunshine striking this
   Alchemize its dullness,
When the sleek curls manifold
Flash all over into gold
   With a burnished fullness.

IV

Underneath my stroking hand,
Startled eyes of hazel bland
   Kindling, growing larger,
Up thou leapest with a spring,
Full of prank and curveting,
   Leaping like a charger.

Leap! thy broad tail waves a light,
Leap! thy slender feet are bright,
    Canopied in fringes;
Leap! those tasselled ears of thine
Flicker strangely, fair and fine
    Down their golden inches.

VI

Yet, my pretty, sportive friend,
Little is't to such an end
    That I praise thy rareness;
Other dogs may be thy peers
Haply in these drooping ears
    And this glossy fairness.

VII

But of *thee* it shall be said,
This dog watched beside a bed
    Day and night unweary,
Watched within a curtained room
Where no sunbeam brake the gloom
    Round the sick and dreary.

VIII

Roses, gathered for a vase,
In that chamber died apace,
    Beam and breeze resigning;
This dog only, waited on,
Knowing that when light is gone
    Love remains for shining.

IX

Other dogs in thymy dew
Tracked the hares and followed through
    Sunny moor or meadow;

This dog only, crept and crept
Next a languid cheek that slept,
 Sharing in the shadow.

X

Other dogs of loyal cheer
Bounded at the whistle clear,
 Up the woodside hieing;
This dog only, watched in reach
Of a faintly uttered speech
 Or a louder sighing.

XI

And if one or two quick tears
Dropped upon his glossy ears
 Or a sigh came double,
Up he sprang in eager haste,
Fawning, fondling, breathing fast,
 In a tender trouble.

XII

And this dog was satisfied
If a pale thin hand would glide
 Down his dewlaps sloping—
Which he pushed his nose within,
After—platforming his chin
 On the palm left open.

XIII

This dog, if a friendly voice
Call him now to blither choice
 Than such a chamber-keeping,
"Come out!" praying from the door—
Presseth backward as before,
 Up against me leaping.

— 80 —

XIV

Therefore to this dog will I,
Tenderly not scornfully,
　　Render praise and favor:
With my hand upon his head,
Is my benediction said
　　Therefore and forever.

XV

And because he loves me so,
Better than his kind will do
　　Often man or woman,
Give I back more love again
Than dogs often take of men,
　　Leaning from my Human.

XVI

Blessings on thee, dog of mine,
Pretty collars make thee fine.
　　Sugared milk make fat thee!
Pleasures wag on in thy tail,
Hands of gentle motion fail
　　Nevermore, to pat thee!

XVII

Downy pillow take thy head,
Silken coverlid bestead,
　　Sunshine help thy sleeping!
No fly's buzzing wake thee up,
No man break thy purple cup
　　Set for drinking deep in.

XVIII

Whiskered cats arointed flee,
Sturdy stoppers keep from thee
　　Cologne distillations;

Nuts lie in thy path for stones,
And thy feast-day macaroons
   Turn to daily rations!

XIX

Mock I thee, in wishing weal?—
Tears are in my eyes to feel
   Thou art made so straitly,
Blessing needs must straiten too—
Little canst thou joy or do,
   Thou who lovest *greatly*.

XX

Yet be blessèd to the height
Of all goods and all delight
   Pervious to thy nature;
Only *loved* beyond that line,
With a love that answers thine,
   Loving fellow-creature!

THAT DAY

I

I stand by the river where both of us stood,
And there is but one shadow to darken the flood;
And the path leading to it, where both used to pass,
Has the step of but one to take dew from the grass—
   One forlorn since that day.

II

The flowers of the margin are many to see;
None stoops at my bidding to pluck them for me.
The bird in the alder sings loudly and long:
My low sound of weeping disturbs not his song,
   As thy vow did that day.

III

I stand by the river, I think of the vow;
Oh, calm as the place is, vow-breaker, be thou!
I leave the flower growing, the bird unreproved:
Would I trouble *thee* rather than *them*, my beloved—
   And my lover that day?

IV

Go, be sure of my love, by that treason forgiven;
Of my prayers, by the blessings they win thee from heaven;
Of my grief (guess the length of the sword by the sheath's)
By the silence of life, more pathetic than death's!
   Go—be clear of that day!

LOVED ONCE

I

I classed, appraising once,
Earth's lamentable sounds—the welladay,
  The jarring yea and nay,
The fall of kisses on unanswering clay,
The sobbed farewell, the welcome mournfuller;
  But all did leaven the air
With a less bitter leaven of sure despair
  Than these words, "I loved *once*."

II

And who saith "I loved *once*"?
Not angels, whose clear eyes, love, love, foresee,
  Love, through eternity,
And by *To Love* to apprehend *To Be*.
Not God, called Love, his noble crown-name casting
  A light too broad for blasting:
The great God changing not from everlasting,
  Saith never, "I loved *once*."

III

Oh, never is "Loved *once*"
Thy word, thou Victim-Christ, misprizèd friend!
  Thy cross and curse may rend,
But, having loved, thou lovest to the end.
This is man's saying—man's: too weak to move
  One spherèd star above,
Man desecrates the eternal God-word Love
  By his No More and Once.

How say ye, "We loved once,"
Blasphemers? Is your earth not cold enow,
   Mourners, without that snow?
Ah, friends, and would ye wrong each other so?
And could ye say of some whose love is known,
   Whose prayers have met your own,
Whose tears have fallen for you, whose smiles have shown
   So long, "We loved them *once*"?

V

Could ye, "We loved her once,"
Say calm of me, sweet friends, when out of sight?
   When hearts of better right
Stand in between me and your happy light?
Or when, as flowers kept too long in the shade,
   Ye find my colors fade,
And all that is not love in me decayed?
   Such words—ye loved me *once!*

Could ye, "We loved her once,"
Say cold of me when further put away
   In earth's sepulchral clay,
When mute the lips which deprecate today?
Not so! not then—least then! When life is shriven,
   And death's full joy is given,
Of those who sit and love you up in heaven,
   Say not "We loved them once."

Say never, ye loved *once:*
God is too near above, the grave, beneath,
   And all our moments breathe
Too quick in mysteries of life and death

For such a word. The eternities avenge
   Affections light of range.
There comes no change to justify that change,
   Whatever comes—Loved *once!*

VIII

   And yet that same word *once*
Is humanly acceptive. Kings have said,
   Shaking a discrowned head,
"We ruled once"—dotards, "We once taught and led";
Cripples once danced i' the vines; and bards approved
   Were once by scornings moved:
But love strikes one hour—*love!* those *never* loved
   Who dream that they loved *once.*

CATARINA TO CAMOENS

DYING IN HIS ABSENCE ABROAD, AND REFERRING TO THE POEM IN WHICH HE RECORDED THE SWEETNESS OF HER EYES

I

On the door you will not enter,
   I have gazed too long—adieu!
Hope withdraws her peradventure—
   Death is near me—and not *you*.
      Come, O lover,
      Close and cover
These poor eyes, you called, I ween,
"Sweetest eyes, were ever seen."

II

When I heard you sing that burden
   In my vernal days and bowers,
Other praises disregarding,
   I but hearkened that of yours—
      Only saying
      In heart-playing,
"Blessed eyes mine eyes have been,
If the sweetest, HIS have seen!"

III

But all changes. At this vesper,
   Cold the sun shines down the door.
If you stood there, would you whisper
   "Love, I love you," as before—

Death pervading
Now, and shading
Eyes you sang of, that yestreen,
As the sweetest ever seen?

IV

Yes, I think, were you beside them,
  Near the bed I die upon—
Though their beauty you denied them,
  As you stood there, looking down,
    You would truly
    Call them duly,
For the love's sake found therein—
"Sweetest eyes, were ever seen."

V

And if *you* looked down upon them,
  And if *they* looked up to *you,*
All the light which has foregone them
  Would be gathered back anew.
    They would truly
    Be as duly
Love-transformed to beauty's sheen—
"Sweetest eyes, were ever seen."

VI

But, ah me! you only see me,
  In your thoughts of loving man,
Smiling soft perhaps and dreamy
  Through the wavings of my fan—
    And unweeting
    Go repeating,
In your reverie serene,
"Sweetest eyes, were ever seen."

VII

While my spirit leans and reaches
    From my body still and pale,
Fain to hear what tender speech is
    In your love to help my bale—
        O my poet,
        Come and show it!
Come, of latest love, to glean
"Sweetest eyes, were ever seen."

VIII

O my poet, O my prophet,
    When you praised their sweetness so,
Did you think, in singing of it,
    That it might be near to go?
        Had you fancies
        From their glances,
That the grave would quickly screen
"Sweetest eyes, were ever seen"?

IX

No reply! the fountain's warble
    In the courtyard sounds alone.
As the water to the marble
    So my heart falls with a moan
        From love-sighing
        To this dying.
Death forerunneth Love to win
"Sweetest eyes, were ever seen."

X

Will you come? When I'm departed
    Where all sweetnesses are hid;
Where thy voice, my tenderhearted,

Will not lift up either lid.
        Cry, O lover,
        Love is over!
Cry beneath the cypress green—
"Sweetest eyes, were ever seen."

XI

When the angelus is ringing,
    Near the convent will you walk,
And recall the choral singing
    Which brought angels down our talk?
        Spirit-shriven
        I viewed Heaven,
Till you smiled—"Is earth unclean,
Sweetest eyes, were ever seen?"

XII

When beneath the palace lattice,
    You ride slow as you have done,
And you see a face there—that is
    Not the old familiar one—
        Will you oftly
        Murmur softly,
"Here, ye watched me morn and e'en,
Sweetest eyes, were ever seen"?

XIII

When the palace ladies, sitting
    Round your gittern, shall have said,
"Poet, sing those verses written
    For the lady who is dead,"
        Will you tremble,
        Yet dissemble—
Or sing hoarse, with tears between,
"Sweetest eyes, were ever seen"?

XIV

"Sweetest eyes!" how sweet in flowings
   The repeated cadence
Though you sang a hundred poems,
   Still the best one would be this.
      I can hear it
      'Twixt my spirit
And the earth-noise intervene—
"Sweetest eyes, were ever seen!"

XV

But the priest waits for the praying,
   And the choir are on their knees,
And the soul must pass away in
   Strains more solemn high than these.
      Miserere
      For the weary!
Oh, no longer for Catrine,
"Sweetest eyes, were ever seen!"

XVI

Keep my ribbon, take and keep it
   (I have loosed it from my hair),
Feeling, while you overweep it,
   Not alone in your despair,
      Since with saintly
      Watch unfaintly
Out of heaven shall o'er you lean
"Sweetest eyes, were ever seen."

XVII

But—but *now*—yet unremovèd
   Up to Heaven, they glisten fast.
You may cast away, Belovèd,
   In your future all my past.

Such old phrases
May be praises
For some fairer bosom-queen—
"Sweetest eyes, were ever seen!"

XVIII

Eyes of mine, what are ye doing?
  Faithless, faithless—praised amiss
If a tear be of your showing,
  Dropped for any hope of HIS!
    Death has boldness
    Besides coldness,
If unworthy tears demean
"Sweetest eyes, were ever seen."

XIX

I will look out to his future;
  I will bless it till it shine.
Should he ever be a suitor
  Unto sweeter eyes than mine,
    Sunshine gild them,
    Angels shield them,
Whatsoever eyes terrene
Be the sweetest HIS have seen!

THE ROMANCE OF THE SWAN'S NEST

I

Little Ellie sits alone
'Mid the beeches of a meadow
  By a stream-side on the grass,
  And the trees are showering down
Doubles of their leaves in shadow
  On her shining hair and face.

II

She has thrown her bonnet by,
And her feet she has been dipping
  In the shallow water's flow;
  Now she holds them nakedly
In her hands, all sleek and dripping,
  While she rocketh to and fro.

III

Little Ellie sits alone,
And the smile she softly uses
  Fills the silence like a speech,
  While she thinks what shall be done—
And the sweetest pleasure chooses
  For her future within reach.

IV

Little Ellie in her smile
Chooses—"I will have a lover,
  Riding on a steed of steeds!
  He shall love me without guile,
And to *him* I will discover
  The swan's nest among the reeds.

V

"And the steed shall be red-roan,
And the lover shall be noble,
　　With an eye that takes the breath;
　　And the lute he plays upon
Shall strike ladies into trouble,
　　As his sword strikes men to death.

VI

"And the steed it shall be shod
All in silver, housed in azure,
　　And the mane shall swim the wind;
　　And the hoofs along the sod
Shall flash onward and keep measure,
　　Till the shepherds look behind.

VII

"But my lover will not prize
All the glory that he rides in,
　　When he gazes in my face:
　　He will say, 'O Love, thine eyes
Build the shrine my soul abides in,
　　And I kneel here for thy grace!'

VIII

"Then, aye, then he shall kneel low,
With the red-roan steed anear him
　　Which shall seem to understand—
　　Till I answer, 'Rise and go!
For the world must love and fear him
　　Whom I gift with heart and hand.'

IX

"Then he will arise so pale,
I shall feel my own lips tremble

With a *yes* I must not say,
  Nathless maiden-brave, 'Farewell,'
I will utter, and dissemble—
  'Light tomorrow with today!'

X

"Then he'll ride among the hills
To the wide world past the river,
  There to put away all wrong;
  To make straight distorted wills,
And to empty the broad quiver
  Which the wicked bear along.

XI

"Three times shall a young foot-page
Swim the stream and climb the mountain
  And kneel down beside my feet—
  'Lo, my master sends this gage,
Lady, for thy pity's counting!
  What wilt thou exchange for it?'

XII

"And the first time, I will send
A white rosebud for a guerdon,
  And the second time, a glove;
  But the third time—I may bend
From my pride, and answer—'Pardon,
  If he comes to take my love.'

XIII

"Then the young foot-page will run,
Then my lover will ride faster,
  Till he kneeleth at my knee:
  'I am a duke's eldest son!
Thousand serfs do call me master—
  But, O Love, I love but *thee!*'

XIV

"He will kiss me on the mouth
Then, and lead me as a lover
   Through the crowds that praise his deeds:
   And, when soul-tied by one troth,
Unto *him* I will discover
   That swan's nest among the reeds."

XV

   Little Ellie, with her smile
Not yet ended, rose up gaily,
   Tied the bonnet, donned the shoe,
   And went homeward round a mile,
Just to see, as she did daily,
   What more eggs were with the two.

XVI

   Pushing through the elm-tree copse,
Winding up the stream, lighthearted,
   Where the osier pathway leads—
   Past the boughs she stoops—and stops.
Lo, the wild swan had deserted,
   And a rat had gnawed the reeds.

XVII

   Ellie went home sad and slow.
If she found the lover ever,
   With his red-roan steed of steeds,
   Sooth I know not! but I know
She could never show him—never,
   That swan's nest among the reeds!

THE DEAD PAN

I

Gods of Hellas, gods of Hellas,
Can ye listen in your silence?
Can your mystic voices tell us
Where ye hide? In floating islands,
With a wind that evermore
Keeps you out of sight of shore?
      Pan, Pan is dead,

II

In what revels are ye sunken
In old Ethiopia?
Have the Pygmies made you drunken,
Bathing in mandragora
Your divine pale lips that shiver
Like the lotus in the river?
      Pan, Pan is dead.

III

Do ye sit there still in slumber,
In gigantic Alpine rows?
The black poppies out of number
Nodding, dripping from your brows
To the red lees of your wine,
And so kept alive and fine?
      Pan, Pan is dead.

IV

Or lie crushed your stagnant corses
Where the silver spheres roll on,

Stung to life by centric forces
Thrown like rays out from the sun?—
While the smoke of your old altars
Is the shroud that round you welters?
Great Pan is dead.

V

"Gods of Hellas, gods of Hellas"
Said the old Hellenic tongue—
Said the hero-oaths, as well as
Poets' songs the sweetest sung:
Have ye grown deaf in a day?
Can ye speak not yea or nay,
Since Pan is dead?

VI

Do ye leave your rivers flowing
All alone, O Naiades,
While your drenchèd locks dry slow in
This cold feeble sun and breeze?
Not a word the Naiads say,
Though the rivers run for aye;
For Pan is dead.

VII

From the gloaming of the oakwood,
O ye Dryads, could ye flee?
At the rushing thunderstroke, would
No sob tremble through the tree?
Not a word the Dryads say,
Though the forests wave for aye;
For Pan is dead.

VIII

Have ye left the mountain places,
Oreads wild, for other tryst?

— 98 —

Shall we see no sudden faces
Strike a glory through the mist?
Not a sound the silence thrills
Of the everlasting hills:
        Pan, Pan is dead.

IX

O twelve gods of Plato's vision,
Crowned to starry wanderings,
With your chariots in procession
And your silver clash of wings!
Very pale ye seem to rise,
Ghosts of Grecian deities,
        Now Pan is dead!

X

Jove, that right hand is unloaded
Whence the thunder did prevail,
While in idiocy of godhead
Thou art staring the stars pale!
And thine eagle, blind and old,
Roughs his feathers in the cold.
        Pan, Pan is dead.

XI

Where, O Juno, is the glory
Of thy regal look and tread?
Will they lay, forevermore, thee
On thy dim, straight, golden bed?
Will thy queendom all lie hid
Meekly under either lid?
        Pan, Pan is dead.

XII

Ha, Apollo! floats his golden
Hair all mist-like where he stands,

While the Muses hang enfolding
Knee and foot with faint wild hands?
'Neath the clanging of thy bow,
Niobe looked lost as thou!
      Pan, Pan is dead.

XIII

Shall the casque with its brown iron
Pallas' broad blue eyes eclipse,
And no hero take inspiring
From the god-Greek of her lips?
'Neath her olive dost thou sit,
Mars the mighty, cursing it?
      Pan, Pan is dead.

XIV

Bacchus, Bacchus! on the panther
He swoons, bound with his own vines;
And his Maenads slowly saunter,
Head aside, among the pines,
While they murmur dreamingly
"Evohe!—ah—evohe!—
      Ah, Pan is dead!"

XV

Neptune lies beside the trident,
Dull and senseless as a stone;
And old Pluto deaf and silent
Is cast out into the sun:
Ceres smileth stern thereat,
"We *all* now are desolate—
      Now Pan is dead."

XVI

Aphrodite! dead and driven
As thy native foam thou art;

With the cestus long done heaving
On the white calm of thine heart!
Ai Adonis! at that shriek
Not a tear runs down her cheek—
      Pan, Pan is dead.

XVII

And the Loves, we used to know from
One another, huddled lie,
Frore as taken in a snowstorm,
Close beside her tenderly;
As if each had weakly tried
Once to kiss her as he died.
      Pan, Pan is dead.

XVIII

What, and Hermes? Time enthralleth
All thy cunning, Hermes, thus,
And the ivy blindly crawleth
Round thy brave caduceus?
Hast thou no new message for us,
Full of thunder and Jove-glories?
      Nay, Pan is dead.

XIX

Crownèd Cybele's great turret
Rocks and crumbles on her head;
Roar the lions of her chariot
Toward the wilderness, unfed:
Scornful children are not mute—
"Mother, mother, walk afoot,
      Since Pan is dead!"

From

Poems of 1850

HECTOR IN THE GARDEN

I

Nine years old! The first of any
    Seem the happiest years that come:
    Yet when *I* was nine, I said
    No such word!—I thought instead
That the Greeks had used as many
    In besieging Ilium.

II

Nine green years had scarcely brought me
    To my childhood's haunted spring:
    I had life, like flowers and bees,
    In betwixt the country trees.
And the sun the pleasure taught me
    Which he teacheth everything.

III

If the rain fell, there was sorrow,
    Little head leant on the pane,
    Little finger drawing down it
    The long trailing drops upon it,
And the "Rain, rain, come tomorrow,"
    Said for charm against the rain.

IV

Such a charm was right Canidian,
    Though you meet it with a jeer!
    If I said it long enough,
    Then the rain hummed dimly off,
And the thrush with his pure Lydian
    Was left only to the ear;

And the sun and I together
  Went a-rushing out of doors!
  We, our tender spirits, drew
  Over hill and dale in view,
Glimmering hither, glimmering thither,
  In the footsteps of the showers.

Underneath the chestnuts dripping,
  Through the grasses wet and fair,
  Straight I sought my garden-ground
  With the laurel on the mound,
And the pear tree oversweeping
  A side-shadow of green air.

In the garden lay supinely
  A huge giant wrought of spade!
  Arms and legs were stretched at length
  In a passive giant strength—
The fine meadow turf, cut finely,
  Round them laid and interlaid.

Call him Hector, son of Priam!
  Such his title and degree:
  With my rake I smoothed his brow,
  Both his cheeks I weeded through,
But a rimer such as I am
  Scarce can sing his dignity.

Eyes of gentianellas azure,
  Staring, winking at the skies;

Nose of gillyflowers and box;
  Scented grasses put for locks,
Which a little breeze, at pleasure,
  Set a-waving round his eyes.

X

Brazen helm of daffodillies,
  With a glitter toward the light;
  Purple violets for the mouth,
  Breathing perfumes west and south;
And a sword of flashing lilies,
  Holden ready for the fight.

XI

And a breastplate made of daisies,
  Closely fitting, leaf on leaf;
  Periwinkles interlaced
  Drawn for belt about the waist;
While the brown bees, humming praises,
  Shot their arrows round the chief.

XII

And who knows (I sometimes wondered)
  If the disembodied soul
  Of old Hector, once of Troy,
  Might not take a dreary joy
Here to enter—if it thundered,
  Rolling up the thunder-roll?

XIII

Rolling this way from Troy-ruin,
  In this body rude and rife
  Just to enter, and take rest
  'Neath the daisies of the breast—
They, with tender roots, renewing
  His heroic heart to life?

— 107 —

XIV

Who could know? I sometimes started
    At a motion or a sound!
    Did his mouth speak—naming Troy,
    With an ὀτοτοτοτι?
Did the pulse of the Strong-hearted
    Make the daisies tremble round?

XV

It was hard to answer, often:
    But the birds sang in the tree—
    But the little birds sang bold
    In the pear-tree green and old,
And my terror seemed to soften
    Through the courage of their glee.

XVI

Oh, the birds, the tree, the ruddy
    And white blossoms, sleek with rain!
    Oh, my garden, rich with pansies!
    Oh, my childhood's bright romances!
All revive, like Hector's body,
    And I see them stir again!

XVII

And despite life's changes—chances,
    And despite the deathbell's toll,
    They press on me in full seeming!
    Help, some angel! stay this dreaming!
As the birds sang in the branches,
    Sing God's patience through my soul!

XVIII

That no dreamer, no neglecter
  Of the present's work unsped,
  I may wake up and be doing,
  Life's heroic ends pursuing,
Though my past is dead as Hector,
  And though Hector is twice dead.

FLUSH OR FAUNUS

You see this dog. It was but yesterday
I mused forgetful of his presence here
Till thought on thought drew downward tear on tear,
When from the pillow where wet-cheeked I lay,
A head as hairy as Faunus thrust its way
Right sudden against my face—two golden-clear
Great eyes astonished mine—a drooping ear
Did flap me on either cheek to dry the spray!
I started first as some Arcadian
Amazed by goatly god in twilight grove,
But as the bearded vision closelier ran
My tears off, I knew Flush, and rose above
Surprise and sadness—thanking the true PAN
Who, by low creatures, leads to heights of love.

MOUNTAINEER AND POET

The simple goatherd between Alp and sky,
Seeing his shadow, in that awful tryst,
Dilated to a giant's on the mist,
Esteems not his own stature larger by
The apparent image, but more patiently
Strikes his staff down beneath his clenching fist,
While the snow-mountains lift their amethyst
And sapphire crowns of splendor, far and nigh,
Into the air around him. Learn from hence
Meek morals, all ye poets that pursue
Your way still onward up to eminence!
Ye are not great because creation drew
Large revelations round your earliest sense,
Nor bright because God's glory shines for you.

HIRAM POWERS' GREEK SLAVE

They say Ideal beauty cannot enter
The house of anguish. On the threshold stands
An alien Image with enshackled hands,
Called the Greek Slave! as if the artist meant her
(That passionless perfection which he lent her,
Shadowed not darkened where the sill expands)
To, so, confront man's crimes in different lands
With man's ideal sense. Pierce to the center,
Art's fiery finger!—and break up ere long
The serfdom of this world! appeal, fair stone,
From God's pure heights of beauty against man's
        wrong!
Catch up in thy divine face, not alone
East griefs but west—and strike and shame the strong,
By thunders of white silence, overthrown.

LIFE

Each creature holds an insular point in space;
Yet what man stirs a finger, breathes a sound,
But all the multitudinous beings round
In all the countless worlds with time and place
For their conditions, down to the central base,
Thrill, haply, in vibration and rebound,
Life answering life across the vast profound,
In full antiphony, by a common grace?
I think this sudden joyaunce which illumes
A child's mouth sleeping, unaware may run
From some soul newly loosened from earth's tombs:
I think this passionate sigh, which half-begun
I stifle back, may reach and stir the plumes
Of God's calm angel standing in the sun.

A SABBATH MORNING AT SEA

I

The ship went on with solemn face;
  To meet the darkness on the deep,
    The solemn ship went onward.
I bowed down weary in the place,
  For parting tears and present sleep
    Had weighed mine eyelids downward.

II

Thick sleep which shut all dreams from me,
  And kept my inner self apart
    And quiet from emotion,
Then brake away and left me free,
  Made conscious of a human heart
    Betwixt the heaven and ocean.

III

The new sight, the new wondrous sight!
  The waters round me, turbulent—
    The skies impassive o'er me,
Calm, in a moonless, sunless light,
  Half glorified by that intent
    Of holding the day-glory!

IV

Two pale thin clouds did stand upon
  The meeting line of sea and sky,
    With aspect still and mystic.
I think they did foresee the sun,
  And rested on their prophecy
    In quietude majestic,

V

Then flushed to radiance where they stood,
  Like statues by the open tomb
  Of shining saints half risen—
The sun!—he came up to be viewed,
  And sky and sea made mighty room
  To inaugurate the vision.

VI

I oft had seen the dawnlight run,
  As red wine, through the hills, and break
  Through many a mist's inurning;
But, here, no earth profaned the sun!
  Heaven, ocean, did alone partake
  The sacrament of morning.

VII

Away with thoughts fantastical!
  I would be humble to my worth,
  Self-guarded as self-doubted:
Though here no earthly shadows fall,
  I, joying, grieving without earth,
  May desecrate without it.

VIII

God's sabbath morning sweeps the waves;
  I would not praise the pageant high,
  Yet miss the dedicature.
I, carried toward the sunless graves
  By force of natural things—should I
  Exult in only nature?

IX

And could I bear to sit alone
  'Mid nature's fixed benignities,
  While my warm pulse was moving?

Too dark thou art, O glittering sun,
  Too strait ye are, capacious seas,
    To satisfy the loving!

X

It seems a better lot than so,
  To sit with friends beneath the beech,
    And feel them dear and dearer;
Or follow children as they go
  In pretty pairs, with softened speech,
    As the churchbells ring nearer.

XI

Love me, sweet friends, this sabbath day!
  The sea sings round me while ye roll
    Afar the hymn unaltered,
And kneel, where once I knelt to pray,
  And bless me deeper in the soul,
    Because the voice has faltered.

XII

And though this sabbath comes to me
  Without the stolèd minister
    Or chanting congregation,
God's spirit brings communion, HE
  Who brooded soft on waters drear,
    Creator on creation.

XIII

Himself, I think, shall draw me higher,
  Where keep the saints with harp and song
    An endless sabbath morning,
And on that sea commixed with fire
  Oft drop their eyelids, raised too long
    To the full Godhead's burning.

A WOMAN'S SHORTCOMINGS

I

She has laughed as softly as if she sighed,
　　She has counted six, and over,
Of a purse well filled and a heart well tried—
　　Oh, each a worthy lover!
They "give her time"; for her soul must slip
　　Where the world has set the grooving.
She will lie to none with her fair red lip—
　　But love seeks truer loving.

II

She trembles her fan in a sweetness dumb,
　　As her thoughts were beyond recalling,
With a glance for *one,* and a glance for *some,*
　　From her eyelids rising and falling;
Speaks common words with a blushful air,
　　Hears bold words, unreproving;
But her silence says—what she never will swear—
　　And love seeks better loving.

III

Go, lady, lean to the night-guitar
　　And drop a smile to the bringer,
Then smile as sweetly, when he is far,
　　At the voice of an indoor singer.
Bask tenderly beneath tender eyes;
　　Glance lightly, on their removing;
And join new vows to old perjuries—
　　But dare not call it loving.

IV

Unless you can think, when the song is done,
　No other is soft in the rhythm;
Unless you can feel, when left by One,
　That all men else go with him;
Unless you can know, when unpraised by his breath,
　That your beauty itself wants proving;
Unless you can swear "For life, for death!"—
　Oh, fear to call it loving!

V

Unless you can muse in a crowd all day
　On the absent face that fixed you;
Unless you can love, as the angels may,
　With the breadth of heaven betwixt you;
Unless you can dream that his faith is fast,
　Through behoving and unbehoving;
Unless you can *die* when the dream is past—
　Oh, never call it loving!

A MAN'S REQUIREMENTS

I

Love me, sweet, with all thou art,
    Feeling, thinking, seeing—
Love me in the lightest part,
    Love me in full being.

II

Love me with thine open youth
    In its frank surrender;
With the vowing of thy mouth,
    With its silence tender.

III

Love me with thine azure eyes,
    Made for earnest granting!
Taking color from the skies,
    Can Heaven's truth be wanting?

IV

Love me with their lids, that fall
    Snowlike at first meeting:
Love me with thine heart, that all
    The neighbors then see beating.

V

Love me with thine hand stretched out
    Freely—open-minded:
Love me with thy loitering foot—
    Hearing one behind it.

Love me with thy voice, that turns
   Sudden faint above me;
Love me with thy blush that burns
   When I murmur "Love me!"

Love me with thy thinking soul—
   Break it to love-sighing;
Love me with thy thoughts that roll
   On through living—dying.

Love me with thy gorgeous airs,
   When the world has crowned thee!
Love me, kneeling at thy prayers,
   With the angels round thee.

Love me pure, as musers do,
   Up the woodlands shady:
Love me gaily, fast, and true,
   As a winsome lady.

Through all hopes that keep us brave,
   Further off or nigher,
Love me for the house and grave—
   And for something higher.

Thus, if thou wilt prove me, dear,
   Woman's love no fable,
I will love *thee*—half-a-year—
   As a man is able.

CHANGE UPON CHANGE

I

Five months ago the stream did flow,
    The lilies bloomed within the sedge,
And we were lingering to and fro,
Where none will track thee in this snow,
    Along the stream beside the hedge.
Ah, Sweet, be free to love and go!
    For if I do not hear thy foot,
    The frozen river is as mute,
    The flowers have dried down to the root.
    And why, since these be changed since May,
      Shouldst *thou* change less than *they?*

II

And slow, slow as the winter snow
    The tears have drifted to mine eyes;
And my poor cheeks, five months ago
Set blushing at thy praises so,
    Put paleness on for a disguise.
All Sweet, be free to praise and go!
    For if my face is turned too pale,
    It was thine oath that first did fail—
    It was thy love proved false and frail!
    And why, since these be changed enow,
      Should *I* change less than *thou?*

A DENIAL

I

We have met late—it is too late to meet,
  O friend, not more than friend!
Death's forecome shroud is tangled round my feet,
And if I step or stir, I touch the end.
  In this last jeopardy
Can I approach thee, I, who cannot move?
How shall I answer thy request for love?
  Look in my face and see.

II

I love thee not, I dare not love thee! Go
  In silence; drop my hand.
If thou seek roses, seek them where they blow
In garden-alleys, not in desert sand.
  Can life and death agree,
That thou shouldst stoop thy song to my complaint?
I cannot love thee. If the word is faint,
  Look in my face and see.

III

I might have loved thee in some former days.
  Oh, then, my spirits had leapt
As now they sink, at hearing thy love-praise!
Before these faded cheeks were overwept,
  Had this been asked of me,
To love thee with my whole strong heart and head,
I should have said still . . . yes, but *smiled* and said,
  "Look in my face and see!"

IV

But now . . . God sees me, God, who took my heart
  And drowned it in life's surge.

In all your wide warm earth I have no part—
A light song overcomes me like a dirge.
    Could Love's great harmony
The saints keep step to when their bonds are loose,
Not weigh me down? am I a wife to choose?
    Look in my face and see—

V

While I behold, as plain as one who dreams,
    Some woman of full worth,
Whose voice, as cadenced as a silver stream's,
Shall prove the fountain-soul which sends it forth;
    One younger, more thought-free
And fair and gay, than I, thou must forget,
With brighter eyes than these . . . which are not wet . . .
    Look in my face and see!

VI

So farewell thou, whom I have known too late
    To let thee come so near.
Be counted happy while men call thee great,
And one belovèd woman feels thee dear!—
    Not I—that cannot be.
I am lost, I am changed—I must go farther, where
The change shall take me worse, and no one dare
    Look in my face and see.

VII

Meantime I bless thee. By these thoughts of mine
    I bless thee from all such!
I bless thy lamp to oil, thy cup to wine,
Thy hearth to joy, thy hand to an equal touch
    Of loyal troth. For me,
I love thee not, I love thee not!—away!
Here's no more courage in my soul to say
    "Look in my face and see."

QUESTION AND ANSWER

I

Love you seek for, presupposes
    Summer heat and sunny glow.
Tell me, do you find moss-roses
    Budding, blooming in the snow?
Snow might kill the rose tree's root—
Shake it quickly from your foot,
    Lest it harm you as you go.

II

From the ivy where it dapples
    A gray ruin, stone by stone—
Do you look for grapes or apples,
    Or for sad green leaves alone?
Pluck the leaves off, two or three—
Keep them for morality
    When you shall be safe and gone.

Sonnets from
the Portuguese

I

I thought once how Theocritus had sung
Of the sweet years, the dear and wished-for years,
Who each one in a gracious hand appears
To bear a gift for mortals, old or young:
And, as I mused it in his antique tongue,
I saw, in gradual vision through my tears,
The sweet, sad years, the melancholy years,
Those of my own life, who by turns had flung
A shadow across me. Straightway I was 'ware,
So weeping, how a mystic Shape did move
Behind me, and drew me backward by the hair;
And a voice said in mastery, while I strove—
"Guess now who holds thee?"—"Death," I said. But,
    there,
The silver answer rang—"Not Death, but Love."

II

But only three in all God's universe
Have heard this word thou hast said—Himself, beside
Thee speaking, and me listening! and replied
One of us . . . *that* was God, . . . and laid the curse
So darkly on my eyelids, as to amerce
My sight from seeing thee—that if I had died,
The deathweights, placed there, would have signified
Less absolute exclusion. "Nay" is worse
From God than from all others, O my friend!
Men could not part us with their worldly jars,
Nor the seas change us, nor the tempests bend;
Our hands would touch for all the mountain bars:
And, heaven being rolled between us at the end,
We should but vow the faster for the stars.

III

Unlike are we, unlike, O princely Heart!
Unlike our uses and our destinies.
Our ministering two angels look surprise
On one another, as they strike athwart
Their wings in passing. Thou, bethink thee, art
A quest for queens to social pageantries,
With gages from a hundred brighter eyes
Than tears even can make mine, to play thy part
Of chief musician. What hast *thou* to do
With looking from the lattice-lights at me,
A poor, tired, wandering singer, singing through
The dark, and leaning up a cypress tree?
The chrism is on thine head—on mine, the dew—
And Death must dig the level where these agree.

IV

Thou hast thy calling to some palace floor,
Most gracious singer of high poems! where
The dancers will break footing, from the care
Of watching up thy pregnant lips for more.
And dost thou lift this house's latch too poor
For hand of thine? and canst thou think and bear
To let thy music drop here unaware
In folds of golden fullness at my door?
Look up and see the casement broken in,
The bats and owlets builders in the roof!
My cricket chirps against thy mandolin.
Hush, call no echo up in further proof
Of desolation! there's a voice within
That weeps . . . as thou must sing . . . alone, aloof.

V

I lift my heavy heart up solemnly,
As once Electra her sepulchral urn,
And, looking in thine eyes, I overturn
The ashes at thy feet. Behold and see
What a great heap of grief lay hid in me,
And how the red wild sparkles dimly burn
Through the ashen grayness. If thy foot in scorn
Could tread them out to darkness utterly,
It might be well perhaps. But if instead
Thou wait beside me for the wind to blow
The gray dust up . . . those laurels on thine head
O my Belovèd, will not shield thee so,
That none of all the fires shall scorch and shred
The hair beneath. Stand farther off then! go.

VI

Go from me. Yet I feel that I shall stand
Henceforward in thy shadow. Nevermore
Alone upon the threshold of my door
Of individual life, I shall command
The uses of my soul, nor lift my hand
Serenely in the sunshine as before,
Without the sense of that which I forbore—
Thy touch upon the palm. The widest land
Doom takes to part us, leaves thy heart in mine
With pulses that beat double. What I do
And what I dream include thee, as the wine
Must taste of its own grapes. And when I sue
God for myself, He hears that name of thine,
And sees within my eyes the tears of two.

VII

The face of all the world is changed, I think,
Since first I heard the footsteps of thy soul
Move still, oh, still, beside me, as they stole
Betwixt me and the dreadful outer brink
Of obvious death, where I, who thought to sink,
Was caught up into love, and taught the whole
Of life in a new rhythm. The cup of dole
God gave for baptism, I am fain to drink,
And praise its sweetness, Sweet, with thee anear.
The names of country, heaven, are changed away
For where thou art or shalt be, there or here;
And this . . . this lute and song . . . loved yesterday,
(The singing angels know) are only dear
Because thy name moves right in what they say.

VIII

What can I give thee back, O liberal
And princely giver, who hast brought the gold
And purple of thine heart, unstained, untold,
And laid them on the outside of the wall
For such as I to take or leave withal,
In unexpected largesse? am I cold,
Ungrateful, that for these most manifold
High gifts, I render nothing back at all?
No so; not cold—but very poor instead.
Ask God who knows. For frequent tears have run
The colors from my life, and left so dead
And pale a stuff, it were not fitly done
To give the same as pillow to thy head.
Go farther! let it serve to trample on.

IX

Can it be right to give what I can give?
To let thee sit beneath the fall of tears
As salt as mine, and hear the sighing years
Re-sighing on my lips renunciative
Through those infrequent smiles which fail to live
For all thy adjurations? O my fears,
That this can scarce be right! We are not peers,
So to be lovers; and I own, and grieve,
That givers of such gifts as mine are, must
Be counted with the ungenerous. Out, alas!
I will not soil thy purple with my dust,
Nor breathe my poison on thy Venice-glass,
Nor give thee any love—which were unjust.
Beloved, I only love thee! let it pass.

X

Yet, love, mere love, is beautiful indeed
And worthy of acceptation. Fire is bright,
Let temple burn, or flax; an equal light
Leaps in the flame from cedar plank or weed:
And love is fire. And when I say at need
I love thee . . . mark! . . . *I love thee*—in thy sight
I stand transfigured, glorified aright,
With conscience of the new rays that proceed
Out of my face toward thine. There's nothing low
In love, when love the lowest: meanest creatures
Who love God, God accepts while loving so.
And what I *feel*, across the inferior features
Of what I *am*, doth flash itself, and show
How that great work of Love enhances Nature's.

XI

And therefore if to love can be desert,
I am not all unworthy. Cheeks as pale
As these you see, and trembling knees that fail
To bear the burden of a heavy heart—
This weary minstrel life that once was girt
To climb Aornus, and can scarce avail
To pipe now 'gainst the valley nightingale
A melancholy music—why advert
To these things? O Belovèd, it is plain
I am not of thy worth nor for thy place!
And yet, because I love thee, I obtain
From that same love this vindicating grace,
To live on still in love, and yet in vain—
To bless thee, yet renounce thee to thy face.

XII

Indeed this very love which is my boast,
And which, when rising up from breast to brow,
Doth crown me with a ruby large enow
To draw men's eyes and prove the inner cost—
This love even, all my worth, to the uttermost,
I should not love withal, unless that thou
Hadst set me an example, shown me how,
When first thine earnest eyes with mine were crossed,
And love called love. And thus, I cannot speak
Of love even, as a good thing of my own:
Thy soul hath snatched up mine all faint and weak,
And placed it by thee on a golden throne—
And that I love (O soul, we must be meek!)
Is by thee only, whom I love alone.

XIII

And wilt thou have me fasten into speech
The love I bear thee, finding words enough,
And hold the torch out, while the winds are rough,
Between our faces, to cast light on each?—
I drop it at thy feet. I cannot teach
My hand to hold my spirit so far off
From myself—me—that I should bring thee proof
In words, of love hid in me out of reach.
Nay, let the silence of my womanhood
Commend my woman-love to thy belief—
Seeing that I stand unwon, however wooed,
And rend the garment of my life, in brief,
By a most dauntless, voiceless fortitude,
Lest one touch of this heart convey its grief.

XIV

If thou must love me, let it be for naught
Except for love's sake only. Do not say
"I love her for her smile—her look—her way
Of speaking gently—for a trick of thought
That falls in well with mine, and certes brought
A sense of pleasant ease on such a day"—
For these things in themselves, Belovèd, may
Be changed, or change for thee—and love, so wrought,
May be unwrought so. Neither love me for
Thine own dear pity's wiping my cheeks dry—
A creature might forget to weep, who bore
Thy comfort long, and lose thy love thereby!
But love me for love's sake, that evermore
Thou mayst love on, through love's eternity.

XV

Accuse me not, beseech thee, that I wear
Too calm and sad a face in front of thine;
For we two look two ways, and cannot shine
With the same sunlight on our brow and hair.
On me thou lookest with no doubting care,
As on a bee shut in a crystalline;
Since sorrow hath shut me safe in love's divine,
And to spread wing and fly in the outer air
Were most impossible failure, if I strove
To fail so. But I look on thee—on thee—
Beholding, besides love, the end of love,
Hearing oblivion beyond memory;
As one who sits and gazes from above,
Over the rivers to the bitter sea.

XVI

And yet, because thou overcomest so,
Because thou art more noble and like a king,
Thou canst prevail against my fears and fling
Thy purple round me, till my heart shall grow
Too close against thine heart henceforth to know
How it shook when alone. Why, conquering
May prove as lordly and complete a thing
In lifting upward, as in crushing low!
And as a vanquished soldier yields his sword
To one who lifts him from the bloody earth,
Even so, Belovèd, I at last record,
Here ends my strife. If *thou* invite me forth,
I rise above abasement at the word.
Make thy love larger to enlarge my worth.

XVII

My poet, thou canst touch on all the notes
God set between His After and Before,
And strike up and strike off the general roar
Of the rushing worlds a melody that floats
In a serene air purely. Antidotes
Of medicated music, answering for
Mankind's forlornest uses, thou canst pour
From thence into their ears. God's will devotes
Thine to such ends, and mine to wait on thine.
How, Dearest, wilt thou have me for most use?
A hope, to sing—by gladly? or a fine
Sad memory, with thy songs to interfuse?
A shade, in which to sing—of palm or pine?
A grave, on which to rest from singing? Choose.

XVIII

I never gave a lock of hair away
To a man, Dearest, except this to thee,
Which now upon my fingers thoughtfully,
I ring out to the full brown length and say
"Take it." My day of youth went yesterday;
My hair no longer bounds to my foot's glee,
Nor plant I it from rose or myrtle tree,
As girls do, anymore: it only may
Now shade on two pale cheeks the mark of tears,
Taught drooping from the head that hangs aside
Through sorrow's trick. I thought the funeral-shears
Would take this first, but Love is justified—
Take it thou—finding pure, from all those years,
The kiss my mother left here when she died.

XIX

The soul's Rialto hath its merchandise;
I barter curl for curl upon that mart,
And from my poet's forehead to my heart
Receive this lock which outweighs argosies,
As purply black, as erst to Pindar's eyes
The dim purpureal tresses gloomed athwart
The nine white Muse-brows. For this counterpart,
The bay-crown's shade, Belovèd, I surmise,
Still lingers on thy curl, it is so black!
Thus, with a fillet of smooth-kissing breath,
I tie the shadows safe from gliding back,
And lay the gift where nothing hindereth;
Here on my heart, as on thy brow, to lack
No natural heat till mine grows cold in death.

XX

Belovèd, my Belovèd, when I think
That thou wast in the world a year ago,
What time I sat alone here in the snow
And saw no footprint, heard the silence sink
No moment at thy voice, but, link by link,
Went counting all my chains as if that so
They never could fall off at any blow
Struck by thy possible hand—why, thus I drink
Of life's great cup of wonder! Wonderful,
Never to feel thee thrill the day or night
With personal act or speech—not ever cull
Some prescience of thee with the blossoms white
Thou sawest growing! Atheists are as dull,
Who cannot guess God's presence out of sight.

XXI

Say over again, and yet once over again,
That thou dost love me. Though the word repeated
Should seem "a cuckoo-song," as thou dost treat it,
Remember, never to the hill or plain,
Valley and wood, without her cuckoo-strain
Comes the fresh Spring in all her green completed.
Belovèd, I, amid the darkness greeted
By a doubtful spirit-voice, in that doubt's pain
Cry, "Speak once more—thou lovest!" Who can fear
Too many stars, though each in heaven shall roll,
Too many flowers, though each shall crown the year?
Say thou dost love me, love me, love me—toll
The silver iterance!—only minding, Dear,
To love me also in silence with thy soul.

XXII

When our two souls stand up erect and strong,
Face to face, silent, drawing nigh and nigher,
Until the lengthening wings break into fire
At either curvèd point—what bitter wrong
Can the earth do to us, that we should not long
Be here contented? Think. In mounting higher,
The angels would press on us and aspire
To drop some golden orb of perfect song
Into our deep, dear silence. Let us stay
Rather on earth, Belovèd—where the unfit
Contrarious moods of men recoil away
And isolate pure spirits, and permit
A place to stand and love in for a day,
With darkness and the death-hour rounding it.

XXIII

Is it indeed so? If I lay here dead,
Wouldst thou miss any life in losing mine?
And would the sun for thee more coldly shine
Because of grave-damps falling round my head?
I marveled, my Belovèd, when I read
Thy thought so in the letter. I am thine—
But . . . *so* much to thee? Can I pour thy wine
While my hands tremble? Then my soul, instead
Of dreams of death, resumes life's tower range.
Then, love me, Love! look on me—breathe on me!
As brighter ladies do not count it strange,
For love, to give up acres and degree,
I yield the grave for thy sake, and exchange
My near sweet view of Heaven, for earth with thee!

XXIV

Let the world's sharpness, like a clasping knife,
Shut in upon itself and do no harm
In this close hand of Love, now soft and warm,
And let us hear no sound of human strife
After the click of the shutting. Life to life—
I lean upon thee, Dear, without alarm,
And feel as safe as guarded by a charm
Against the stab of worldlings, who if rife
Are weak to injure. Very whitely still
The lilies of our lives may reassure
Their blossoms from their roots, accessible
Alone to heavenly dews that drop not fewer,
Growing straight, out of man's reach, on the hill.
God only, who made us rich, can make us poor.

XXV

A heavy heart, Belovèd, have I borne
From year to year until I saw thy face,
And sorrow after sorrow took the place
Of all those natural joys as lightly worn
As the stringed pearls, each lifted in its turn
By a beating heart at dance-time. Hopes apace
Were changed to long despairs, till God's own grace
Could scarcely lift above the world forlorn
My heavy heart. Then *thou* didst bid me bring
And let it drop adown thy calmly great
Deep being! Fast it sinketh, as a thing
Which its own nature doth precipitate,
While thine doth close above it, mediating
Betwixt the stars and the unaccomplished fate.

XXVI

I lived with visions for my company
Instead of men and women, years ago,
And found them gentle mates, nor thought to know
A sweeter music than they played to me.
But soon their trailing purple was not free
Of this world's dust, their lutes did silent grow,
And I myself grew faint and blind below
Their vanishing eyes. Then *thou* didst come—to be,
Belovèd, what they seemed. Their shining fronts,
Their songs, their splendors (better, yet the same,
As river water hallowed into fonts),
Met in thee, and from out thee overcame
My soul with satisfaction of all wants:
Because God's gifts put man's best dreams to shame.

XXVII

My own Belovèd, who has lifted me
From this drear flat of earth where I was thrown,
And, in betwixt the languid ringlets, blown
A life-breath, till the forehead hopefully
Shines out again, as all the angels see,
Before thy saving kiss! My own, my own,
Who camest to me when the world was gone,
And I who looked for only God, found *thee!*
I find thee; I am safe, and strong, and glad.
As one who stands in dewless asphodel
Looks backward on the tedious time he had
In the upper life—so I, with bosom-swell,
Make witness, here, between the good and bad,
That Love, as strong as Death, retrieves as well.

XXVIII

My letters! all dead paper, mute and white!
And yet they seem alive and quivering
Against my tremulous hands which loose the string
And let them drop down on my knee tonight.
This said—he wished to have me in his sight
Once, as a friend: this fixed a day in spring
To come and touch my hand . . . a simple thing,
Yes I wept for it!—this . . . the paper's light . . .
Said, *Dear, I love thee;* and I sank and quailed
As if God's future thundered on my past.
This said, *I am thine*—and so its ink has paled
With lying at my heart that beat too fast.
And this . . . O Love, thy words have ill availed
If, what this said, I dared repeat at last!

XXIX

I think of thee!—my thoughts do twine and bud
About thee, as wild vines, about a tree,
Put out broad leaves, and soon there's naught to see
Except the straggling green which hides the wood.
Yet, O my palm tree, be it understood
I will not have my thoughts instead of thee
Who art dearer, better! Rather, instantly
Renew thy presence; as a strong tree should,
Rustle thy boughs and set thy trunk all bare,
And let these bands of greenery which insphere thee
Drop heavily down—burst, shattered, everywhere!
Because, in this deep joy to see and hear thee
And breathe within thy shadow a new air,
I do not think of thee—I am too near thee.

XXX

I see thine image through my tears tonight
And yet today I saw thee smiling. How
Refer the cause?—Belovèd, is it thou
Or I, who makes me sad? The acolyte
Amid the chanted joy and thankful rite
May so fall flat, with pale insensate brow,
On the altar stair. I hear thy voice and vow,
Perplexed, uncertain, since thou art out of sight,
As he, in his swooning ears, the choir's Amen.
Belovèd, dost thou love? or did I see all
The glory as I dreamed, and fainted when
Too vehement light dilated my ideal,
For my soul's eyes? Will that light come again,
As now these tears come—falling hot and real?

XXXI

Thou comest! all is said without a word.
I sit beneath thy looks, as children do
In the noon-sun, with souls that tremble through
Their happy eyelids from an unaverred
Yet prodigal inward joy. Behold, I erred
In that last doubt! and yet I cannot rue
The sin most, but the occasion—that we two
Should for a moment stand unministered
By a mutual presence. Ah, keep near and close,
Thou dovelike help! and, when my fears would rise,
With thy broad heart serenely interpose:
Brood down with thy divine sufficiencies
These thoughts which tremble when bereft of those,
Like callow birds left desert to the skies.

XXXII

The first time that the sun rose on thine oath
To love me, I looked forward to the moon
To slacken all those bonds which seemed too soon
And quickly tied to make a lasting troth.
Quick-loving hearts, I thought, may quickly loathe;
And, looking on myself, I seemed not one
For such man's love!—more like an out-of-tune
Worn viol, a good singer would be wroth
To spoil his song with, and which, snatched in haste,
Is laid down at the first ill-sounding note.
I did not wrong myself so, but I placed
A wrong on *thee*. For perfect strains may float
'Neath master-hands, from instruments defaced—
And great souls, at one stroke, may do and dote.

XXXIII

Yes, call me by my pet-name! let me hear
The name I used to run at, when a child,
From innocent play, and leave the cowslips piled,
To glance up in some face that proved me dear
With the look of its eyes. I miss the clear
Fond voices which, being drawn and reconciled
Into the music of Heaven's undefiled,
Call me no longer. Silence on the bier,
While I call God—call God!—So let thy mouth
Be heir to those who are now exanimate.
Gather the north flowers to complete the south,
And catch the early love up in the late.
Yes, call me by that name—and I, in truth,
With the same heart, will answer and not wait.

XXXIV

With the same heart, I said, I'll answer thee
As those, when thou shalt call me by my name—
Lo, the vain promise! is the same, the same,
Perplexed and ruffled by life's strategy?
When called before, I told how hastily
I dropped my flowers or brake off from a game,
To run and answer with the smile that came
At play last moment, and went on with me
Through my obedience. When I answer now,
I drop a grave thought, break from solitude;
Yet still my heart goes to thee—ponder how—
Not as to a single good, but all my good!
Lay thy hand on it, best one, and allow
That no child's foot could run fast as this blood.

XXXV

If I leave all for thee, wilt thou exchange
And be all to me? Shall I never miss
Home-talk and blessing and the common kiss
That comes to each in turn, nor count it strange,
When I look up, to drop on a new range
Of walls and floors, another home than this?
Nay, wilt thou fill that place by me which is
Filled by dead eyes too tender to know change?
That's hardest. If to conquer love, has tried,
To conquer grief, tries more, as all things prove;
For grief indeed is love and grief beside.
Alas, I have grieved so I am hard to love.
Yet love me—wilt thou? Open thine heart wide,
And fold within the wet wings of thy dove.

XXXVI

When we met first and loved, I did not build
Upon the event with marble. Could it mean
To last, a love set pendulous between
Sorrow and sorrow? Nay, I rather thrilled,
Distrusting every light that seemed to gild
The onward path, and feared to overlean
A finger even. And, though I have grown serene
And strong since then, I think that God has willed
A still renewable fear . . . O love, O troth . . .
Lest these enclaspèd hands should never hold,
This mutual kiss drop down between us both
As an unowned thing, once the lips being cold.
And Love, be false! if *he*, to keep one oath,
Must lose one joy, by his life's star foretold.

XXXVII

Pardon, oh, pardon, that my soul should make,
Of all that strong divineness which I know
For thine and thee, an image only so
Formed of the sand, and fit to shift and break.
It is that distant years which did not take
Thy sovereignty, recoiling with a blow,
Have forced my swimming brain to undergo
Their doubt and dread, and blindly to forsake
Thy purity of likeness and distort
Thy worthiest love to a worthless counterfeit:
As if a shipwrecked Pagan, safe in port,
His guardian sea-god to commemorate,
Should set a sculptured porpoise, gills a-snort
And vibrant tail, within the temple gate.

XXXVIII

First time he kissed me, he but only kissed
The fingers of this hand wherewith I write;
And ever since, it grew more clean and white,
Slow to world-greetings, quick with its "Oh, list,"
When the angels speak. A ring of amethyst
I could not wear here, plainer to my sight,
Than that first kiss. The second passed in height
The first, and sought the forehead, and half missed,
Half falling on the hair. O beyond meed!
That was the chrism of love, which love's own crown,
With sanctifying sweetness, did precede.
The third upon my lips was folded down
In perfect, purple state; since when, indeed,
I have been proud and said, "My love, my own."

XXXIX

Because thou hast the power and own'st the grace
To look through and behind this mask of me
(Against which years have beat thus blanchingly
With their rains), and behold my soul's true face,
The dim and weary witness of life's race—
Because thou hast the faith and love to see,
Through that same soul's distracting lethargy,
The patient angel waiting for a place
In the new Heavens—because nor sin nor woe,
Nor God's infliction, nor death's neighborhood,
Nor all which others viewing, turn to go,
Nor all which makes me tired of all, self-viewed—
Nothing repels thee . . . Dearest, teach me so
To pour out gratitude, as thou dost, good!

XL

Oh, yes! they love through all this world of ours!
I will not gainsay love, called love forsooth.
I have heard love talked in my early youth,
And since, not so long back but that the flowers
Then gathered, smell still. Mussulmans and Giaours
Throw kerchiefs at a smile, and have no ruth
For any weeping. Polypheme's white tooth
Slips on the nut if, after frequent showers,
The shell is over-smooth—and not so much
Will turn the thing called love, aside to hate
Or else to oblivion. But thou art not such
A lover, my Belovèd! thou canst wait
Through sorrow and sickness, to bring souls to touch,
And think it soon when others cry "Too late."

XLI

I thank all who have loved me in their hearts,
With thanks and love from mine. Deep thanks to all
Who paused a little near the prison wall
To hear my music in its louder parts
Ere they went onward, each one to the mart's
Or temple's occupation, beyond call.
But thou, who, in my voice's sink and fall
When the sob took it, thy divinest Art's
Own instrument didst drop down at thy foot
To hearken what I said between my tears . . .
Instruct me how to thank thee! Oh, to shoot
My soul's full meaning into future years,
That *they* should lend it utterance, and salute
Love that endures, from Life that disappears!

XLII

"My future will not copy fair my past"—
I wrote that once; and thinking at my side
My ministering life-angel justified
The word by his appealing look upcast
To the white throne of God, I turned at last,
And there, instead, saw thee, not unallied
To angels in thy soul! Then I, long tried
By natural ills, received the comfort fast,
While budding, at thy sight, my pilgrim's staff
Gave out green leaves with morning dews impearled.
I seek no copy now of life's first half:
Leave here the pages with long musing curled,
And write me new my future's epigraph,
New angel mine, unhoped for in the world!

XLIII

How do I love thee? Let me count the ways.
I love thee to the depth and breadth and height
My soul can reach, when feeling out of sight
For the ends of Being and ideal Grace.
I love thee to the level of everyday's
Most quiet need, by sun and candlelight.
I love thee freely, as men strive for Right;
I love thee purely, as they turn from Praise.
I love thee with the passion put to use
In my old griefs, and with my childhood's faith.
I love thee with a love I seemed to lose
With my lost saints—I love thee with the breath,
Smiles, tears, of all my life!—and, if God choose,
I shall but love thee better after death.

XLIV

Belovèd, thou hast brought me many flowers
Plucked in the garden, all the summer through
And winter, and it seemed as if they grew
In this close room, nor missed the sun and showers.
So, in the like name of that love of ours,
Take back these thoughts which here unfolded too,
And which on warm and cold days I withdrew
From my heart's ground. Indeed, those beds and bowers
Be overgrown with bitter weeds and rue,
And wait thy weeding; yet here's eglantine,
Here's ivy!—take them, as I used to do
Thy flowers, and keep them where they shall not pine.
Instruct thine eyes to keep their colors true,
And tell thy soul their roots are left in mine.

From

Casa Guidi
Windows

CASA GUIDI WINDOWS

A Poem in Two Parts

FROM PART I

I heard last night a little child go singing
   'Neath Casa Guidi windows, by the church,
O bella libertà, O bella!—stringing
   The same words still on notes he went in search
So high for, you concluded the upspringing
   Of such a nimble bird to sky from perch
Must leave the whole bush in a tremble green,
   And that the heat of Italy must beat,
While such a voice had leave to rise serene
   'Twixt church and palace of a Florence street:
A little child, too, who not long had been
   By mother's finger steadied on his feet,
And still *O bella libertà* he sang.

Then I thought, musing, of the innumerous
   Sweet songs which still for Italy outrang
From older singers' lips who sang not thus
   Exultingly and purely, yet with pang
Fast sheathed in music, touched the heart of us
   So finely that the pity scarcely pained.
I thought how Filicaja led on others,
   Bewailers for their Italy enchained,
And how they called her childless among mothers,
   Widow of empires, ay, and scarce refrained
Cursing her beauty to her face, as brothers
   Might a shamed sister's—"Had she been less fair
She were less wretched"—how, evoking so
   From congregated wrong and heaped despair

Of men and women writhing under blow,
   Harrowed and hideous in a filthy lair,
Some personating Image wherein woe
   Was wrapped in beauty from offending much,
They called it Cybele, or Niobe,
   Or laid it corpselike on a bier for such,
Where all the world might drop for Italy
   Those cadenced tears which burn not where they touch—
"Juliet of nations, canst thou die as we?
   And was the violet crown that crowned thy head
So overlarge, though new buds made it rough,
   It slipped down and across thine eyelids dead,
O sweet, fair Juliet?" Of such songs enough,
   Too many of such complaints! behold, instead,
Void at Verona, Juliet's marble trough:
   As void as that is, are all images
Men set between themselves and actual wrong,
   To catch the weight of pity, meet the stress
Of conscience—since 'tis easier to gaze long
   On mournful masks and sad effigies
Than on real, live, weak creatures crushed by strong.

          ✿   ✿   ✿

I do believe, divinest Angelo,
   That winter-hour in Via Larga, when
They bade thee build a statue up in snow
   And straight that marvel of thine art again
Dissolved beneath the sun's Italian glow,
   Thine eyes, dilated with the plastic passion,
Thawing too in drops of wounded manhood, since,
   To mock alike thine art and indignation,
Laughed at the palace window the new prince—
   ("Aha! this genius needs for exaltation,
When all's said and howe'er the proud may wince,
   A little marble from our princely mines!")
I do believe that hour thou laughedst too

For the whole sad world and for thy Florentines,
After those few tears, which were only few!
That as, beneath the sun, the grand white lines
Of thy snow-statue trembled and withdrew—
The head, erect as Jove's, being palsied first,
The eyelids flattened, the full brow turned blank,
The right hand, raised but now as if it cursed,
Dropped, a mere snowball, (till the people sank
Their voices, though a louder laughter burst
From the royal window)—thou couldst proudly thank
God and the prince for promise and presage,
And laugh the laugh back, I think verily,
Thine eyes being purged by tears of righteous rage
To read a wrong into a prophecy,
And measure a true great man's heritage
Against a mere great duke's posterity.
I think thy soul said then, "I do not need
A princedom and its quarries, after all;
For if I write, paint, carve a word, indeed,
On book or board or dust, on floor or wall,
The same is kept of God who taketh heed
That not a letter of the meaning fall
Or ere it touch and teach His world's deep heart,
Outlasting, therefore, all your lordships, sir!
So keep your stone, beseech you, for your part,
To cover up your grave-place and refer
The proper titles; I live by my art.
The thought I threw into this snow shall stir
This gazing people when their gaze is done;
And the tradition of your act and mine,
When all the snow is melted in the sun,
Shall gather up, for unborn men, a sign
Of what is the true princedom—ay, and none
Shall laugh that day, except the drunk with wine."

From Casa Guidi windows I looked out,
Again looked and beheld a different sight.
    The Duke had fled before the people's shout
"Long live the Duke!" A people, to speak right,
    Must speak as soft as courtiers, lest a doubt
Should curdle brows of gracious sovereigns, white.
    Moreover that same dangerous shouting meant
Some gratitude for future favors, which
    Were only promised, the Constituent
Implied, the whole being subject to the hitch
    In "motu proprios," very incident
To all these Czars, from Paul to Paulovitch.
    Whereat the people rose up in the dust
Of the ruler's flying feet, and shouted still
    And loudly; only, this time, as was just,
Not "Live the Duke," who had fled for good or ill,
    But "Live the People," who remained and must,
The unrenounced and unrenounceable.
    Long live the people! How they lived! and boiled
And bubbled in the cauldron of the street:
    How the young blustered, nor the old recoiled,
And what a thunderous stir of tongues and feet
    Trod flat the palpitating bells and foiled
The joy-guns of their echo, shattering it!
    How down they pulled the Duke's arms everywhere!
How up they set new café-signs, to show
    Where patriots might sip ices in pure air—
(The fresh paint smelling somewhat)! To and fro
    How marched the civil guard, and stopped to stare
When boys broke windows in a civic glow!
    How rebel songs were sung to loyal tunes,
And bishops cursed in ecclesiastic meters:
    How all the Circoli grew large as moons,
And all the speakers, moonstruck—thankful greeters

Of prospects which struck poor the ducal boons,
A mere free Press, and Chambers!—frank repeaters
    Of great Guerazzi's praises—"There's a man,
The father of the land, who, truly great,
    Takes off that national disgrace and ban,
The farthing tax upon our Florence-gate,
    And saves Italia as he only can!"
How all the nobles fled, and would not wait,
    Because they were most noble—which being so,
How Liberals vowed to burn their palaces,
    Because free Tuscans were not free to go!
How grown men raged at Austria's wickedness,
    And smoked—while fifty striplings in a row
Marched straight to Piedmont for the wrong's redress!
    You say we failed in duty, we who wore
Black velvet like Italian democrats,
    Who slashed our sleeves like patriots, nor forswore
The true republic in the form of hats?
    We chased the archbishop from the Duomo door,
We chalked the walls with bloody caveats
    Against all tyrants. If we did not fight
Exactly, we fired muskets up the air
    To show that victory was ours of right.
We met, had free discussion everywhere
    (Except perhaps i' the Chambers) day and night.
We proved the poor should be employed . . . that's fair—
    And yet the rich not worked for anywise—
Pay certified, yet payers abrogated—
    Full work secured, yet liabilities
To overwork excluded—not one bated
    Of all our holidays, that still, at twice
Or thrice a week, are moderately rated.
    We proved that Austria was dislodged, or would
Or should be, and that Tuscany in arms
    Should, would dislodge her, ending the old feud;
And yet, to leave our piazzas, shops, and farms,

For the simple sake of fighting, was not good—
We proved that also. "Did we carry charms
  Against being killed ourselves, that we should rush
On killing others? what, desert herewith
  Our wives and mothers?—was that duty? tush!"
At which we shook the sword within the sheath
  Like heroes—only louder; and the flush
Ran up the cheek to meet the future wreath.
  Nay, what we proved, we shouted—how we shouted
(Especially the boys did), boldly planting
  That tree of liberty, whose fruit is doubted,
Because the roots are not of nature's granting!
  A tree of good and evil: none, without it,
Grow gods; alas and, with it, men are wanting!

From

Aurora Leigh

"There it is!—
You play beside a deathbed like a child,
Yet measure to yourself a prophet's place
To teach the living. None of all these things
Can women understand. You generalize
Oh, nothing—not even grief! Your quick-breathed hearts,
So sympathetic to the personal pang,
Close on each separate knife-stroke, yielding up
A whole life at each wound, incapable
Of deepening, widening a large lap of life
To hold the world-full woe. The human race
To you means, such a child, or such a man,
You saw one morning waiting in the cold,
Beside that gate, perhaps. You gather up
A few such cases, and when strong sometimes
Will write of factories and of slaves, as if
Your father were a negro, and your son
A spinner in the mills. All's yours and you,
All, colored with your blood, or otherwise
Just nothing to you. Why, I call you hard
To general suffering. Here's the world half-blind
With intellectual light, half-brutalized
With civilization, having caught the plague
In silks from Tarsus, shrieking east and west
Along a thousand railroads, mad with pain
And sin too! . . . does one woman of you all
(You who weep easily) grow pale to see
This tiger shake his cage?—does one of you
Stand still from dancing, stop from stringing pearls,
And pine and die because of the great sum
Of universal anguish?—Show me a tear

Wet as Cordelia's, in eyes bright as yours,
Because the world is mad. You cannot count,
That you should weep for this account, not you!
You weep for what you know. A red-haired child
Sick in a fever, if you touch him once,
Though but so little as with a fingertip,
Will set you weeping; but a million sick . . .
You could as soon weep for the rule of three
Or compound fractions. Therefore, this same world,
Uncomprehended by you, must remain
Uninfluenced by you—Women as you are,
Mere women, personal and passionate,
You give us doting mothers, and perfect wives,
Sublime Madonnas, and enduring saints!
We get no Christ from you—and verily
We shall not get a poet, in my mind."
"With which conclusion you conclude" . . .

                                        "But this,"
That you, Aurora, with the large live brow
And steady eyelids, cannot condescend
To play at art, as children play at swords,
To show a pretty spirit, chiefly admired
Because true action is impossible.
You never can be satisfied with praise
Which men give women when they judge a book
Not as mere work but as mere woman's work,
Expressing the comparative respect
Which means the absolute scorn. "Oh, excellent.
What grace, what facile turns, what fluent sweeps,
What delicate discernment . . . almost thought!
The book does honor to the sex, we hold.
Among our female authors we make room
For this fair writer, and congratulate
The country that produces in these times
Such women, competent to . . . spell."

                                        "Stop there,"

I answered, burning through his thread of talk
With a quick flame of emotion—"You have read
My soul, if not my book, and argue well
I would not condescend . . . we will not say
To such a kind of praise (a worthless end
Is praise of all kinds), but to such a use
Of holy art and golden life. I am young,
And peradventure weak—you tell me so—
Through being a woman. And, for all the rest,
Take thanks for justice. I would rather dance
At fairs on a tightrope, till the babies dropped
Their gingerbread for joy—than shift the types
For tolerable verse, intolerable
To men who act and suffer. Better far
Pursue a frivolous trade by serious means,
Than a sublime art frivolously."

                    *   *   *

With quiet indignation I broke in,
"You misconceive the question like a man,
Who sees a woman as the complement
Of his sex merely. You forget too much
That every creature, female as the male,
Stands single in responsible act and thought
As also in birth and death. Whoever says
To a loyal woman, 'Love and work with me,'
Will get fair answers if the work and love,
Being good themselves, are good for her—the best
She was born for. Women of a softer mood,
Surprised by men when scarcely awake to life,
Will sometimes only hear the first word, love,
And catch up with it any kind of work,
Indifferent, so that dear love go with it.
I do not blame such women, though, for love,
They pick much oakum; earth's fanatics make

— 161 —

Too frequently heaven's saints. But *me* your work
Is not the best for—nor your love the best,
Nor able to commend the kind of work
For love's sake merely."

FROM BOOK VII

I found a house at Florence on the hill
Of Bellosguarda. 'Tis a tower which keeps
A post of double observation o'er
That valley of Arno (holding as a hand
The outspread city) straight towards Fiesole
And Mount Morello and the setting sun,
The Vallombrosan mountains opposite,
Which sunrise fills as full as crystal cups
Turned red to the brim because their wine is red.
No sun could die nor yet be born unseen
By dwellers at my villa: morn and eve
Were magnified before us in the pure
Illimitable space and pause of sky,
Intense as angels' garments blanched with God,
Less blue than radiant. From the outer wall
Of the garden, drops the mystic floating gray
Of olive trees (with interruptions green
from maize and vine), until 'tis caught and torn
Upon the abrupt black line of cypresses
Which signs the way to Florence. Beautiful
The city lies along the ample vale,
Cathedral, tower and palace, piazza and street,
The river trailing like a silver cord
Through all, and curling loosely, both before
And after, over the whole stretch of land
Sown whitely up and down its opposite slopes
With farms and villas.

But oh, the night! oh, bittersweet! oh, sweet!
O Dark, O moon and stars, O ecstasy
Of darkness! O great mystery of love,
In which absorbed, loss, anguish, treason's self
Enlarges rapture—as a pebble dropped
In some full wine cup overbrims the wine!
While we two sat together, leaned that night
So close my very garments crept and thrilled
With strange electric life, and both my cheeks
Grew red, then pale, with touches from my hair
In which his breath was—while the golden moon
Was hung before our faces as the badge
Of some sublime inherited despair,
Since ever to be seen by only one—
A voice said, low and rapid as a sigh,
Yet breaking, I felt conscious, from a smile
"Thank God, who made me blind, to make me see!
Shine on, Aurora, dearest light of souls,
Which rul'st forevermore both day and night!
I am happy."

From

Last Poems

A FALSE STEP

I

Sweet, thou hast trod on a heart,
  Pass; there's a world full of men;
And women as fair as thou art
  Must do such things now and then.

II

Thou only hast stepped unaware;
  Malice, not one can impute;
And why should a heart have been there,
  In the way of a fair woman's foot?

III

It was not a stone that could trip,
  Nor was it a thorn that could rend:
Put up thy proud underlip!
  'Twas merely the heart of a friend.

IV

And yet, peradventure, one day
  Thou, sitting alone at the glass,
Remarking the bloom gone away,
  Where the smile in its dimplement was,

V

And seeking around thee in vain,
  From hundreds who flattered before,
Such a word as, "Oh, not in the main
  Do I hold thee less precious, but more!". . .

VI

Thou'lt sigh, very like, on thy part,
   "Of all I have known or can know,
I wish I had only that heart
   I trod upon ages ago!"

LORD WALTER'S WIFE

I

"But why do you go," said the lady, while both sat under the
   yew,
And her eyes were alive in their depth, as the kraken beneath
   the sea-blue.

II

"Because I fear you," he answered—"because you are far too
   fair,
And able to strangle my soul in a mesh of your gold-colored
   hair."

III

"Oh, that," she said, "is no reason! Such knots are quickly
   undone,
And too much beauty, I reckon, is nothing but too much sun."

IV

"Yet farewell so," he answered—"the sunstroke's fatal at
   times.
I value your husband, Lord Walter, whose gallop rings still
   from the limes."

V

"Oh, that," she said, "is no reason. You smell a rose through a
   fence:
If two should smell it, what matters? who grumbles, and
   where's the pretense?"

"But I," he replied, "have promised another, when love
    was free,
To love her alone, alone, who alone and afar loves me."

"Why, that," she said, "is no reason. Love's always free, I am
    told.
Will you vow to be safe from the headache on Tuesday, and
    think it will hold?"

"But you," he replied, "have a daughter, a young little child,
    who was laid
In your lap to be pure; so, I leave you: the angels would make
    me afraid."

"Oh, that," she said, "is no reason. The angels keep out of the
    way;
And Dora, the child, observes nothing, although you should
    please me and stay."

At which he rose up in his anger—"Why, now, you no longer
    are fair!
Why, now, you no longer are fatal, but ugly and hateful, I
    swear."

At which she laughed out in her scorn—"These men! Oh,
    these men overnice,
Who are shocked if a color, not virtuous, is frankly put on by
    a vice."

XII

Her eyes blazed upon him—"And *you!* You bring us your
    vices so near
That we smell them! You think in our presence a thought
    'twould defame us to hear!

XIII

"What reason had you, and what right—I appeal to your soul
    from my life—
To find me too fair as a woman? Why, sir, I am pure, and
    a wife.

XIV

"Is the daystar too fair up above you? It burns you not. Dare
    you imply
I brushed you more close than the star does, when Walter
    had set me as high?

XV

"If a man finds a woman too fair, he means simply adapted
    too much
To uses unlawful and fatal. The praise!—shall I thank you for
    such?

XVI

"Too fair?—not unless you misuse us! and surely if, once
    in a while,
You attain to it, straightway you call us no longer too fair, but
    too vile.

XVII

"A moment? I pray your attention!—I have a poor word in
    my head
I must utter, though womanly custom would set it down
    better unsaid.

XVIII

"You grew, sir, pale to impertinence, once when I showed
you a ring.
You kissed my fan when I dropped it. No matter!—I've
broken the thing.

XIX

"You did me the honor, perhaps, to be moved at my side
now and then
In the senses—a vice, I have heard, which is common to
beasts and some men.

XX

"Love's a virtue for heroes!—as white as the snow on high
hills,
And immortal as every great soul is that struggles, endures,
and fulfills.

XXI

"I love my Walter profoundly—you, Maude, though you
faltered a week,
For the sake of . . . what was it? an eyebrow? or, less still,
a mole on a cheek?

XXII

"And since, when all's said, you're too noble to stoop to the
frivolous cant
About crimes irresistible, virtues that swindle, betray and
supplant,

XXIII

"I determined to prove to yourself that, whate'er you might
dream or avow
By illusion, you wanted precisely no more of me than you
have now.

XXIV

"There! look me full in the face!—in the face. Understand, if
    you can,
That the eyes of such women as I am, are clean as the palm
    of a man.

XXV

"Drop his hand, you insult him. Avoid us for fear we should
    cost you a scar—
You take us for harlots, I tell you, and not for the women we
    are.

XXVI

"You wronged me: but then I considered . . . there's Walter!
    And so at the end,
I vowed that he should not be mulcted, by me, in the hand
    of a friend.

XXVII

"Have I hurt you indeed? We are quits then. Nay, friend of
    my Walter, be mine!
Come Dora, my darling, my angel, and help me to ask him
    to dine."

BIANCA AMONG THE NIGHTINGALES

I

The cypress stood up like a church
    That night we felt our love would hold,
And saintly moonlight seemed to search
    And wash the whole world clean as gold;
The olives crystallized the vales'
    Broad slopes until the hills grew strong:
The fireflies and the nightingales
    Throbbed each to either, flame and song.
The nightingales, the nightingales.

II

Upon the angle of its shade
    The cypress stood, self-balanced high;
Half up, half down, as double made,
    Along the ground, against the sky.
And *we* too! from such soul-height went
    Such leaps of blood, so blindly driven,
We scarce knew if our nature meant
    Most passionate earth or intense heaven.
The nightingales, the nightingales.

III

We paled with love, we shook with love,
    We kissed so close we could not vow;
Till Giulio whispered, "Sweet, above
    God's Ever guarantees this Now."
And through his words the nightingales
    Drove straight and full their long clear call,
Like arrows through heroic mails,
    And love was awful in it all.
The nightingales, the nightingales.

IV

O cold white moonlight of the north,
  Refresh these pulses, quench this hell!
O coverture of death drawn forth
  Across this garden-chamber . . . well!
But what have nightingales to do
  In gloomy England, called the free . . .
(Yes, free to die in! . . .) when we two
  Are sundered, singing still to me?
And still they sing, the nightingales.

I think I hear him, how he cried
  "My own soul's life" between their notes.
Each man has but one soul supplied,
  And that's immortal. Though his throat's
On fire with passion now, to *her*
  He can't say what to me he said!
And yet he moves her, they aver.
  The nightingales sing through my head,
The nightingales, the nightingales.

VI

He says to *her* what moves her most.
  He would not name his soul within
Her hearing—rather pays her cost
  With praises to her lips and chin.
Man has but one soul, 'tis ordained,
  And each soul but one love, I add;
Yet souls are damned and love's profaned.
  These nightingales will sing me mad!
The nightingales, the nightingales.

I marvel how the birds can sing.
  There's little difference, in their view,

Betwixt our Tuscan trees that spring
   As vital flames into the blue,
And dull round blots of foliage meant
   Like saturated sponges here
To suck the fogs up. As content
   Is *he* too in this land, 'tis clear.
And still they sing, the nightingales.

VIII

My native Florence! dear, foregone!
   I see across the Alpine ridge
How the last feast day of St. John
   Shot rockets from Carraia bridge.
The luminous city, tall with fire,
   Trod deep down in that river of ours,
While many a boat with lamp and choir
   Skimmed birdlike over glittering towers.
I will not hear these nightingales.

IX

I seem to float, *we* seem to float
   Down Arno's stream in festive guise;
A boat strikes flame into our boat
   And up that lady seems to rise
As then she rose. The shock had flashed
   A vision on us! What a head,
What leaping eyeballs!—beauty dashed
   To splendor by a sudden dread.
And still they sing, the nightingales.

X

Too bold to sin, too weak to die;
   Such women are so. As for me,
I would we had drowned there, he and I,
   That moment, loving perfectly.
He had not caught her with her loosed
   Gold ringlets . . . rarer in the south . . .

Nor heard the "Grazie tanto" bruised
  To sweetness by her English mouth.
And still they sing, the nightingales.

XI

She had not reached him at my heart
  With her fine tongue, as snakes indeed
Kill flies; nor had I, for my part,
  Yearned after, in my desperate need,
And followed him as he did her
  To coasts left bitter by the tide,
Whose very nightingales, elsewhere
  Delighting, torture and deride!
For still they sing, the nightingales.

XII

A worthless woman! mere cold clay
  As all false things are! but so fair,
She takes the breath of men away
  Who gaze upon her unaware.
I would not play her larcenous tricks
  To have her looks! She lied and stole,
And spat into my lover's pure pyx
  The rank saliva of her soul.
And still they sing, the nightingales.

XIII

I would not for her white and pink,
  Though such he likes—her grace of limb,
Though such he has praised—nor yet, I think,
  For life itself, though spent with him,
Commit such sacrilege, affront
  God's nature which is love, intrude
'Twixt two affianced souls, and hunt
  Like spiders, in the altar's wood.
I cannot bear these nightingales.

XIV

If she chose sin, some gentler guise
   She might have sinned in, so it seems:
She might have pricked out both my eyes,
   And I still seen him in my dreams!
—Or drugged me in my soup or wine,
   Nor left me angry afterward:
To die here with his hand in mine
   His breath upon me, were not hard.
(Our Lady hush these nightingales!)

But set a springe for *him,* "mio ben,"
   My only good, my first last love!—
Though Christ knows well what sin is, when
   He sees some things done they must move
Himself to wonder. Let her pass.
   I think of her by night and day.
Must *I* too join her . . . out, alas! . . .
   With Giulio, in each word I say?
And evermore the nightingales!

Giulio, my Giulio!—sing they so,
   And you be silent? Do I speak,
And you not hear? An arm you throw
   Round someone, and I feel so weak?
—Oh, owl-like birds! They sing for spite,
   They sing for hate, they sing for doom!
They'll sing through death who sing through night,
   They'll sing and stun me in the tomb—
The nightingales, the nightingales!

AMY'S CRUELTY

I

Fair Amy of the terraced house,
  Assist me to discover
Why you who would not hurt a mouse
  Can torture so your lover.

II

You give your coffee to the cat,
  You stroke the dog for coming,
And all your face grows kinder at
  The little brown bee's humming.

III

But when *he* haunts your door . . . the town
  Marks coming and marks going . . .
You seem to have stitched your eyelids down
  To that long piece of sewing!

IV

You never give a look, not you,
  Nor drop him a "Good morning,"
To keep his long day warm and blue,
  So fretted by your scorning.

V

She shook her head—"The mouse and bee
  For crumb or flower will linger:
The dog is happy at my knee,
  The cat purrs at my finger.

VI

"But *he* . . . to *him*, the least thing given
　　Means great things at a distance;
He wants my world, my sun, my heaven,
　　Soul, body, whole existence.

VII

"They say love gives as well as takes;
　　But I'm a simple maiden—
My mother's first smile when she wakes
　　I still have smiled and prayed in.

VIII

"I only know my mother's love
　　Which gives all and asks nothing;
And this new loving sets the groove
　　Too much the way of loathing.

IX

"Unless he gives me all in change,
　　I forfeit all things by him:
The risk is terrible and strange—
　　I tremble, doubt . . . deny him.

X

"He's sweetest friend, or hardest foe,
　　Best angel, or worst devil;
I either hate or . . . love him so,
　　I can't be merely civil!

XI

"You trust a woman who puts forth,
　　Her blossoms thick as summer's?

You think she dreams what love is worth,
  Who casts it to newcomers?

XII

"Such love's a cowslip-ball to fling,
  A moment's pretty pastime;
I give . . . all me, if anything,
  The first time and the last time.

XIII

"Dear neighbor of the trellised house,
  A man should murmur never,
Though treated worse than dog and mouse,
  Till doted on forever!"

DE PROFUNDIS

I

The face which, duly as the sun,
Rose up for me with life begun,
To mark all bright hours of the day
With hourly love, is dimmed away—
And yet my days go on, go on.

II

The tongue which, like a stream, could run
Smooth music from the roughest stone,
And every morning with "Good day"
Make each day good, is hushed away—
And yet my days go on, go on.

III

The heart which, like a staff, was one
For mine to lean and rest upon,
The strongest on the longest day
With steadfast love, is caught away—
And yet my days go on, go on.

IV

And cold before my summer's done,
And deaf in Nature's general tune,
And fallen too low for special fear,
And here, with hope no longer here—
While the tears drop, my days go on.

V

The world goes whispering to its own,
"This anguish pierces to the bone";

And tender friends go sighing round,
"What love can ever cure this wound?"
My days go on, my days go on.

VI

The past rolls forward on the sun
And makes all night. O dreams begun,
Not to be ended! Ended bliss,
And life that will not end in this!
My days go on, my days go on.

VII

Breath freezes on my lips to moan:
As one alone, once not alone,
I sit and knock at Nature's door,
Heart-bare, heart-hungry, very poor,
Whose desolated days go on.

VIII

I knock and cry—Undone, undone!
Is there no help, no comfort—none?
No gleaning in the wide wheat-plains
Where others drive their loaded wains?
My vacant days go on, go on.

IX

This Nature, though the snows be down,
Thinks kindly of the bird of June:
The little red hip on the tree
Is ripe for such. What is for me,
Whose days so winterly go on?

X

No bird am I, to sing in June,
And dare not ask an equal boon.
Good nests and berries red are Nature's

To give away to better creatures—
And yet my days go on, go on.

XI

I ask less kindness to be done—
Only to loose these pilgrim-shoon
(Too early worn and grimed), with sweet
Cool deathly touch to these tired feet,
Till days go out which now go on.

XII

Only to lift the turf unmown
From off the earth where it has grown,
Some cubit-space, and say, "Behold,
Creep in, poor Heart, beneath that fold,
Forgetting how the days go on."

XIII

What harm would that do? Green anon
The sward would quicken, overshone
By skies as blue; and crickets might
Have leave to chirp there day and night
While my new rest went on, went on.

XIV

From gracious Nature have I won
Such liberal bounty? may I run
So, lizardlike, within her side,
And there be safe, who now am tried
By days that painfully go on?

XV

—A Voice reproves me thereupon,
More sweet than Nature's when the drone
Of bees is sweetest, and more deep

Than when the rivers overleap
The shuddering pines, and thunder on.

XVI

God's Voice, not Nature's! Night and noon
He sits upon the great white throne
And listens for the creatures' praise.
What babble we of days and days?
The Dayspring He, whose days go on.

XVII

He reigns above, He reigns alone;
Systems burn out and leave His throne:
Fair mists of seraphs melt and fall
Around Him, changeless amid all—
Ancient of Days, whose days go on.

XVIII

He reigns below, He reigns alone,
And, having life in love forgone
Beneath the crown of sovereign thorns,
He reigns the Jealous God. Who mourns
Or rules with Him, while days go on?

XIX

By anguish which made pale the sun,
I hear Him charge His saints that none
Among His creatures anywhere
Blaspheme against Him with despair,
However darkly days go on.

XX

Take from my head the thorn-wreath brown!
No mortal grief deserves that crown.
O súpreme Love, chief Misery,

The sharp regalia are for THEE.
Whose days eternally go on!

XXI

For us—whatever's undergone,
Thou knowest, willest what is done.
Grief may be joy misunderstood;
Only the Good discerns the good.
I trust Thee while my days go on.

XXII

Whatever's lost, it first was won:
We will not struggle nor impugn.
Perhaps the cup was broken here,
That Heaven's new wine might show more clear.
I praise Thee while my days go on.

XXIII

I praise Thee while my days go on;
I love Thee while my days go on:
Through dark and dearth, through fire and frost,
With emptied arms and treasure lost,
I thank Thee while my days go on.

XXIV

And having in Thy life-depth thrown
Being and suffering (which are one),
As a child drops his pebble small
Down some deep well, and hears it fall
Smiling—so I. THY DAYS GO ON.

INDEX OF TITLES AND FIRST LINES

A heavy heart, Belovèd, have I borne   139

Accuse me not, beseech thee, that I wear   134

Amy's Cruelty   179

And therefore if to love can be desert   132

And wilt thou have me fasten into speech   133

And yet, because thou overcomest so   134

Aurora Leigh, From   157

Because thou hast the power and own'st the grace   146

Belovèd, my Belovèd, when I think   136

Belovèd, thou hast brought me many flowers   148

Bianca among the Nightingales   174

But only three in all God's universe   127

"But why do you go," said the lady, while both sat under
     the yew   169

Can it be right to give what I can give?   131

Casa Guidi Windows, From   149

Catarina to Camoens   87

Change upon Change   121

Cowper's Grave   20

Cry of the Children, The   72

De Profundis   182

Dead Pan, The   97

Dear my friend and fellow student   28

Denial, A   122

Do ye hear the children weeping, O my brothers   72

Each creature holds an insular point in space   113

Fair Amy of the terraced house   179

False Step, A   167

First time he kissed me, he but only kissed   145

Five months ago the stream did flow   121

Flush or Faunus   110

Go from me. Yet I feel that I shall stand   129

Gods of Hellas, gods of Hellas   97

Hector in the Garden   105

Hiram Powers' Greek Slave   112

How do I love thee? Let me count the ways.   148

How joyously the young sea-mew   16

I classed, appraising once   84

I lift my heavy heart up solemnly   129

I lived with visions for my company   139

I never gave a lock of hair away   135

I see thine image through my tears tonight   141

I stand by the river where both of us stood   83

I thank all who have loved me in their hearts   147

I think of thee!—my thoughts do twine and bud   141

I thought once how Theocritus had sung   127

If I leave all for thee, wilt thou exchange   144

If thou must love me, let it be for naught   133

In the pleasant orchard closes   56

Indeed this very love which is my boast   132

Is it indeed so? If I lay here dead   138

It is a place where poets crowned may   20

Lady Geraldine's Courtship   28

Lady's Yes, The   54

Let the world's sharpness, like a clasping knife   138

Life   113

Little Ellie sits alone   93

Lord Walter's Wife   169

Lost Bower, The   56

Love me, sweet, with all thou art   119

Love you seek for, presupposes   124
Loved Once   84
Loving friend, the gift of one   78

Man's Requirements, A   119
Mountaineer and Poet   111
"My future will not copy fair my past"—   147
My letters! all dead paper, mute and white!   140
My own Belovèd, who has lifted me   140
My poet, thou canst touch on all the notes   135

Nine years old! The first of any   105

Oh, yes! they love through all this world of ours!   146
On the door you will not enter   87

Pardon, oh, pardon, that my soul should make   145

Question and Answer   124

Romance of the Swan's Nest, The   93

Sabbath Morning at Sea, A   114
Say over again, and yet once over again   137
Sea-Mew, The   16
Seaside Walk, A   18
She has laughed as softly as if she sighed   117
Song, A   15
Sonnets from the Portuguese   125
Soul's Expression, The   27
Sweet, thou hast trod on a heart   167

That Day   83
The cypress stood up like a church   174
The face of all the world is changed, I think   130
The face which, duly as the sun   182
The first time that the sun rose on thine oath   142

The ship went on with solemn face 114
The simple goatherd between Alp and sky 111
The soul's Rialto hath its merchandise 136
They say Ideal beauty cannot enter 112
Thou comest! all is said without a word. 142
Thou hast thy calling to some palace floor 128
To Flush, My Dog 78

Unlike are we, unlike, O princely Heart! 128

We have met late—it is too late to meet 122
We walked beside the sea 18

Weep, as if you thought of laughter! 15
What can I give thee back, O liberal 130
When our two souls stand up erect and strong 137
When we met first and loved, I did not build 144
With stammering lips and insufficient sound 27
With the same heart, I said, I'll answer thee 143
Woman's Shortcomings, A 117

Yes, call me by my pet-name! let me hear 143
"Yes," I answered you last night 54
Yet, love, mere love, is beautiful indeed 131
You see this dog. It was but yesterday 110